DIY
Direct Marketing

DIY
Direct Marketing

An Essential Guide for Beginners

Judith Donovan CBE

KOGAN
PAGE

First published in 2000

Kogan Page Limited
120 Pentonville Road
London N1 9JN
UK

Kogan Page Limited
163 Central Avenue, Suite 4
Dover NH 03820
USA

British Library Cataloguing in Publication Data

A CIP record for this book is available from the British Library.

ISBN 0 7494 3304 3

Typeset by Saxon Graphics Ltd, Derby
Printed and bound in Great Britain by Clays Ltd, St Ives plc

Contents

	About the Author	*vii*
	Introduction	*ix*
1	Direct marketing – science or art?	1
2	Planning your attack	7
3	The media mix	16
4	Please, Mr Postman	26
5	Understanding the list jungle	33
6	Consumer lists	41
7	Yuppies, Dinkys, et al	50
8	Business lists	58
9	A picture is worth a thousand words – not!	67
10	A picture is worth a thousand words – maybe!	77
11	If you touch it, you feel it	85
12	From shoe box to computer: what is a database?	95
13	A nice warm feeling, but . . .	104
14	How to get the best from your media buying	115
15	Generating response from advertising	127
16	Hey, you – I don't know your name	136
17	Bums on seats or bums off seats?	144
18	Does your campaign have the ring of success?	152
19	Web-wise or Web-weary?	160
20	A catalogue of errors or a catalogue of success?	164
21	Measuring direct marketing	173
22	Pot-pourri	177
	Glossary	*189*
	Index	*193*

About the Author

Judith Donovan CBE is the founder and chairman of JDA, one of the older direct marketing agencies in the UK.

Judith's client-side career started with the Ford Motor Company, continued with London advertising agencies such as JWT, and culminated in five years as advertising manager at Grattan. During her period at Grattan, she won the Royds Prize for the highest marks in the CAM Diploma, and was the first holder of the Female Executive of the Year Award.

In 1982, Judith started as a self-employed direct marketing consultant, turning the consultancy into an agency in 1985. That agency now employs 60 people, and handles clients all over the UK in the fields of mail order, financial services, retail, charity, business-to-business services and manufacturing.

Judith has also been active in the wider world of direct marketing. She has been honoured with *UK Direct*'s 'Lifetime Achiever' award and has been included in the Direct Marketing Association's (DMA), Roll of Honour. In 1999 she became the DMA's Chairman, and she is also Editor-in-Chief of *Direct Marketing Strategies*.

As the owner of a small business, Judith has always been deeply involved in civic and business affairs relating to owner-managed SMEs. She was the first Chairman of the Bradford Business Club, chaired the Bradford TEC for nine years, and in 1999 was elected the first-ever female president of Bradford Chamber of Commerce.

Introduction

Welcome! If any of my friends in the industry are reading this, stop now! This book is not for you – you know it all already. This is meant to be a do-it-yourself guide for those setting out to do direct marketing for the first time – whether as small business owners or as beginners in our great and glorious industry.

You *can* do it – it's not that difficult, honestly! For overseas readers, 90 per cent is still relevant – just skip the chapters on profiling and door to door.

Have a good journey!

Direct marketing – science or art?

All good textbooks should start with a definition, and like all good theories there are as many definitions as there are theorists. My own favourite is the following:

'Direct marketing is the science of arresting the human intelligence long enough to take money off it.'

Cynical perhaps, but undoubtedly true. Let me explain. Direct marketing is different from any other type of marketing because it seeks to generate a direct response from pre-identified prospects. 'Ah,' you may say, 'but all marketing does that. That's why companies use TV and press, posters and sales promotion, rep forces and telemarketing.' Indeed, that is so, but the difference with direct marketing is that we can measure its effectiveness in hard cash. We don't have to set up research surveys to see if more people have heard of us after our marketing activity than before. We measure our cost per enquiry, our cost per lead, and ultimately our cost per sale and lifetime value. That's why direct marketing is different.

The phrase 'direct marketing' embraces a number of activities, which will be looked at in more detail over the next few chapters. Let us for the moment, however, stick with the principle – a principle which puts direct marketing at the scientific end of the marketing spectrum. This probably most closely resembles the vision of the philosopher and scientist C.P. Snow, whose 1959 lecture 'The Two Cultures` talked of a marriage of science and the arts fusing into a third culture in the modern world.

The principle of direct marketing does not, however, make it in any way restrictive. In more than 20 years in the industry I have yet to come across a product or service which cannot benefit from the application of direct marketing techniques – direct marketing works for business-to-business, or business-to-consumer, for selling directly, from a catalogue or an advertisement, or for selling indirectly, for example getting people into a retail outlet or getting an appointment for a representative.

Case Study

Dairy Daughters

Product:

Bull semen from the USA, Italy, France and Holland, for artificial insemination, sold direct to UK dairy farmers.

Objectives:

1. To create awareness and impact in the marketplace.
2. To elicit response to register with Dairy Daughters.
3. To build a database of responders for future marketing use.

Challenges:

First-ever mail order service for bull semen for artificial insemination of cattle, so we had to overcome initial distrust of the product. Farmers were used to salesmen calling at their doors, so we had to make the process as simple as possible, to encourage them to order by mail.

Target market:

UK dairy farmers.

Offer:

Better quality, lower-priced semen with guaranteed delivery within 10 working days.

Creative platform:

We played upon farmers' earthy sense of humour, using this throughout the creative on all pieces.

Channels/Media:

1. Direct mail.
2. Inserts.
3. Press ads.

Results:

With an overall response rate of 3.4 per cent, we exceeded our target by 200 per cent!

In addition, the use of direct marketing offers many side benefits, including the following: increasing brand awareness because you are concentrating your message at your target audience and not diluting it at everyone; the generation of a lead file from people who have expressed interest in your proposition but have not actually purchased; the opportunity for cost-effective testing of product, price and positioning; and, last but by no means least, the opportunity to control your marketing expenditure and not have to throw money at walls and hope a bit sticks.

Direct marketing can appear complex and sophisticated – indeed, it has the ability to be extremely clever – but in its simplest form it is the modern-day equivalent of the travelling pedlar. Loading up his pack horse with basic merchandise, the pedlar would travel the length and breadth of the country selling to people he had identified in advance, offering them goods they wanted, needed or desired, and persuading them to purchase via a face-to-face sell conveyed with charm, sincerity and guile.

It is often said that 'people buy people first'. How true that is, but in a mass-market world, very few of us could survive on just face-to-face selling. Direct marketing is a marvellous substitute – it takes your message, your product, your service into the hands of the people you want to talk to, controls the style and force of that message and, ultimately, gives a measurable sale.

No wonder it's such a fast-growing method of selling – and it's one we practise in our daily lives without necessarily realizing it. Jehovah's Witnesses practise direct marketing. Boy Scouts on their Bob a Job week practise direct marketing. A young man setting out to find a girlfriend practises direct marketing. This book will attempt to tell you in practical terms how you too can practise direct marketing for the benefit of your business.

One word of caution: as with any other exclusive club, there is a joining fee. Once you're in, you pay your annual subscription, but in your first year you pay to join. That's the price of your investment in a learning curve to find out what works best for you and how best to exploit it. Hopefully, this book will help you keep that fee to a minimum.

Let me finish this opening with a serious definition: 'Direct marketing is any directly measurable marketing activity which identifies, talks to and signs up prospects, and then turns them into customers of value through ongoing communications.'

2

Planning your attack

You're probably wondering when we are going to get down to the nitty-gritty of direct marketing. 'Tell me about direct mail!', I hear you cry. Well, before we look at the individual elements, we need to establish how to plan first, because the planning disciplines are the same whatever the medium. Indeed, the planning disciplines are the same as for general marketing except that you must be far more precise and accurate in the detail of your planning.

In direct marketing, there are five questions to consider:

- ❑ Whom am I trying to reach?
- ❑ What do I want them to do?
- ❑ Why should they do it?
- ❑ Where should I reach them?
- ❑ When should I reach them?

WHOM AM I TRYING TO REACH?

This is where you define your target market.

To whom do you want to talk? Businesses? Consumers? Both? How are you going to define it further? If it's businesses, is it by type, or number of employees, or turnover, or job title, or a combination? Don't forget that in business-to-business, you can go horizontally or vertically, or both. Horizontal means going after a particular function across a number of industries, for example, company accountants. Vertical means going after one particular industry, for example, chemical engineering. If you want consumers, are you going to use socio-economic and demographic definitions such as ABC1, or are you going to use one of the profiling techniques such as ACORN? Does age matter? Does sex matter? Do you need to identify them by buying habits?

Don't forget that targeting is one of the key benefits of using direct marketing.

Case Study

London Zoo

Product:

London Zoo.

Background:

London Zoo needed to get at London families who might be interested in sponsorship/adoption of animals, which meant they needed to visit the zoo.

Objective:

To generate visits to London Zoo from Londoners.

Challenge:

Small budget.

Target market:

Families living within the bounds of the M25 area of London.

Offer:

Learn more about London Zoo; come and visit us.

Creative platform:

The piece was designed to pull at the heartstrings, with 'lonely hearts' copy. The furry animals had an instant 'ahhh' appeal and a schedule of feeding focused on daily activities.

Channels/Media:

500,000 distributed via door-to-door.

Results:

0.045 per cent response.

WHAT DO I WANT THEM TO DO?

Here we come to the nub of your proposition. What are you selling and how should the recipient of your communication react? Sounds straightforward, but it's amazing how often it is not clear. The first decision you must make is whether the response you want is one-stage or two-stage; do you want an immediate commitment, or just an expression of interest? This is likely to be dictated by what you are selling and at what price. You won't sell new cars or JCBs on a one-stage approach, but you might sell computer peripherals or book collections.

Having decided whether your position is one- or two-stage, you must then work that through to the mechanics of the response. Is it clip a coupon, fill in a reply card, pick up a telephone, go to a Web site, wait to be contacted? Make this absolutely clear to the reader – and think through the logistics yourself. Don't do what one advertiser did recently: he was looking for cheques with order and enclosed a reply paid card – presumably the responder was expected to staple the cheque to the card!

WHY SHOULD THEY DO IT?

This is your corporate and product story. This is where you shout your USP (Unique Selling Proposition). Are you better, cheaper, quicker, larger? Is your company longer-established, a winner of more awards, highly specialist? But it is not where you indulge in a panegyric for your company – we are not on an ego trip. You must turn your company and product features into consumer benefits: 'Our unique umdromic throttle bender will solve your problems with wiggling flanges'; 'Our exciting credit scheme means you can re-furnish your lounge now'.

WHERE SHOULD I REACH THEM?

Here you are defining your target market in geographic terms and media terms. Are you selling to the country as a whole or only in one town or region? Do you need to work with a TV area or a local radio area? Do you have a number of branches for which you want to market within a 5- or 10-mile circle? Is your market the UK only or overseas as well? Is your campaign for existing customers? If so, you'll use your database. If it's customer recruitment, you'll need to decide on your media/channels.

Case Study

NORWEB

Product:

ENERGi – the new brand for both electricity and gas supplied by NORWEB.

Background:

The energy market in Britain was being deregulated and by the end of 1998 domestic consumers were able to choose the supplier from which they bought gas and electricity.

Objective:

To retain electricity customers.

Challenge:

Data protection – NORWEB is not allowed to use its electricity customer billing database to promote gas unless customers have positively opted in to receiving such offers.

Target market:

All existing domestic electricity customers (1.8m).

Offer:

Stage One – Opt in.
Stage Two – Once opted in, open the information pack.

Creative platform:

The creative was heavily branded with the ENERGi brand colours.

The method of circumnavigating the data protection issue, with basically two mailings in one, was both innovative and extremely cost-effective, particularly when mailing to a base of 1.8 million.

Results:

Target cost per contract: £21; actual cost per contract: £5. Exceeded sales target by 400 per cent.

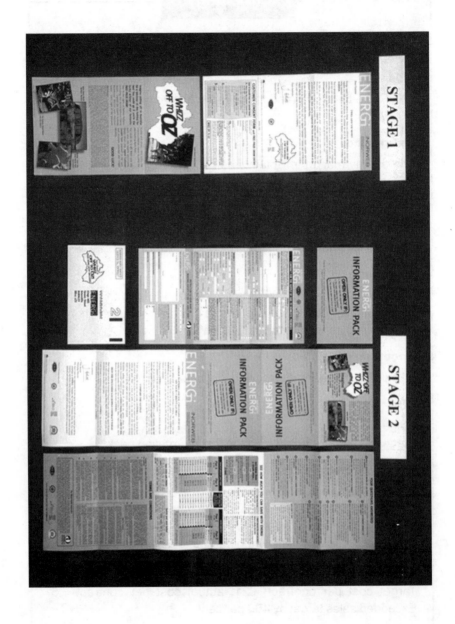

WHEN SHOULD I REACH THEM?

Some products have seasonality built in – others do not. You would not sell Easter eggs in November or fireworks in February. You will know if your product is seasonal. Other products are heavily influenced by the weather. Double-glazing companies get more coupons when the weather is cold. A famous thermal underwear company holds its direct mail until the temperature drops. Perhaps more important for consideration is the day of the week. There is very little point in business-to-business direct marketing appearing at the weekend. Mondays are bad too, as post accumulates over the weekend and much of British industry holds planning meetings on Monday mornings. Equally, many firms close early on Friday.

Conversely, more and more consumers are out at work all day – the UK now has the highest percentage of women working of any country in Europe. Weekend messages are bound to work better – as proved by the success of the Sunday supplements for off-the-page advertisers.

There you have it. Don't spend one penny on direct marketing until you have gone through this planning exercise.

3

The media mix

Still with me so far? We've talked about the principles of direct marketing and the planning process that you must go through. Let's now look at the media: the communications opportunities that exist for applying the principles already identified, often referred to as 'channels'.

Again, there are as many definitions as theories, but the list which we usually work to is as follows:

1. direct mail;
2. direct-response advertising;
3. door-to-door;
4. piggybacks;
5. telemarketing;
6. the Internet;
7. catalogues (also a distribution channel);
8. miscellaneous.

We will look at these in more detail later, but for now let us consider some thumbnail definitions.

DIRECT MAIL

Really the easiest to identify if you think about it. It means writing to someone! A communication goes via the Royal Mail to a recipient who has been pre-identified either by name and address, or just by address. It sounds simple, until you actually try and make it work. Then, a number of elements come into play, all of which require quite a high level of sophistication to achieve success. Imagine the three legs of a stool. The tripod structure allows it to balance, and you should look for the same balance – of list, offer and creative – in direct mail. Of these three, the list is without a doubt the most important. You can send a bad pack to a good list and you'll get some response. A good pack sent to the wrong list will receive no response. Future chapters will look in detail at how to get all these elements right.

Remember, direct mail can sell most things, if done properly.

DIRECT-RESPONSE ADVERTISING

Forget all that advertising – Coca-Cola, Oxo, Ford – you know and love so well. Of course it's good, and it seems to work. We're talking here about advertising that can be measured – because it solicits a direct response from the reader which can be measured on a cost per enquiry/cost per sale basis. All types of advertising are applicable: newspapers, magazines, consumer, business-to-business, and even TV, radio, cinema and posters, although to a lesser extent.

Again, there are rules and tricks for improving response – inserts vs space, with and without coupons, classified vs display. The bottom line is that you can use direct-response advertising in any medium where advertising normally appears. I call it 'reverse targeting' – letting the prospect come to you, rather than you going to the prospect as in direct mail.

DOOR-TO-DOOR

A very powerful way of reaching consumers at home because it is cheap, and how much you pay often determines whether direct marketing is cost-effective for you. Basically, you can use a number of carriers to deliver a message through a consumer letterbox, either on a blanket or a targeted drop. That message can be anything from a 50p-off voucher to a full-blown catalogue pack (with certain weight restrictions).

PIGGYBACKS

'Bouncebacks', 'third parties' and 'swaps' are all terms that are used in the industry. My favourite is 'piggybacks', because that accurately describes this particular opportunity; one company's message is 'piggybacked' on to another company's direct marketing programme. The message can be put in with another company's recruitment mailings, statements, or other correspondence, or put out with another company's 'product dispatch' – the goods they send. Either way, 'piggybacking' provides a degree of targeting within a relatively cost-effective environment.

Case Study

Wedgwood

Product:

Commemorative china and crystal.

Background:

Wedgwood got serious business from companies commissioning special pieces for significant anniversaries. The campaign set out to alert companies with looming anniversaries of the service.

Objectives:

To generate leads, build up the database, raise awareness and sell the product.

Target Market:

Sales and marketing directors.

Offer:

Free Wedgwood cup and saucer if you see a rep.

Creative Platform:

Reflected brand values. Classy and blue.

Channels/Media:

Sales and marketing trade press, and direct mail to a list of companies with 'founding' anniversaries in the next 12 months.

Results:

The campaign brought in new leads and increased the prospect database by 12½ per cent, producing immediate orders.

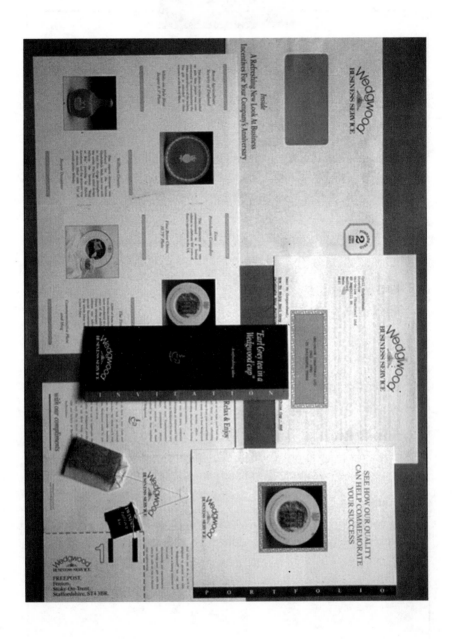

TELEMARKETING

Probably the fastest-growing area within direct marketing involves using the telephone either as a stand-alone or as an integral part of the direct marketing mix. Telemarketing basically splits into inbound and outbound: maximizing telephone calls coming into the organization, whether they be enquiries or sales, or using telephone calls from you to customers or prospective customers to achieve a direct sale or just to open a dialogue.

The disciplines that apply are similar to those in direct mail: you must be able to identify the person to whom you want to talk on the telephone, and to identify accurate telephone numbers. You must then apply the highest standards of professionalism in 'scripting' and communication to maximize what is a powerful but sensitive medium. You must also be aware of the Data Protection Act and the Telephone Preference Service.

THE INTERNET

If it's anything, the Internet is a direct marketing medium. It can function like any advertising medium, providing a location where you create awareness of your product/service and then solicit interested enquiries. Equally, you can engage in full-blown 'e-commerce' – virtual mail order, if you like – where you trade electronically. The golden rule with the Internet is: if you're going to do it, do it well – but do not abandon other forms of trading. The Internet is about additionality, not substitution.

CATALOGUES

An enormous topic in its own right! For many companies, catalogues are an effective substitute for retail or wholesale outlets, giving them total control over the selling process. For other companies, they are an adjunct to main trading either within a retail scenario (very rare), or to back up a rep force. Either way, they work to a set of rules that have nothing to do with normal brochure design, and the catalogue itself is often the tip of the iceberg; without database management and proper systems and controls, you might as well not bother.

MISCELLANEOUS

This covers any direct marketing opportunity not detailed under any of the other headings. This might include leaflets under windscreen wipers, people standing in shopping centres handing out brochures, billboards on top of parked cars, reply cards in local authority material – the opportunities are endless.

Case Study

Tesco Direct

Product:

Tesco *Baby & Toddler* mail-order catalogue.

Objective:

To recruit customers for the mail-order business.

Challenge:

To recruit new mail-order buyers without damaging retail sales from the same audience.

Target market:

Mothers-to-be and parents of babies and toddlers aged up to three years.

Channels/Media:

Two-stage insert in relevant magazines: *Our Baby* – 51,000; *Mother & Baby* – 91,000.

Creative platform:

The two-stage die-cut insert was designed to maximize impact and to carry the offer message in a striking way by using a very cute, endearing baby picture to encourage readers to send for the catalogue.

Results:

Response rate: 8.54 per cent.

4

Please, Mr Postman

We've made it at last to a chapter on direct mail. So where shall we start? I tend to tread carefully with definitions as there are as many definitions of direct mail as there are textbooks on marketing theories.

Direct mail is about writing to people and sending that communication through the postal system, in other words knowing in advance to whom you want to talk, and reaching them via the post. It's a complex subject and I will be devoting several chapters to it.

Let's start with the basic principles. As I've already said, there are three key elements to direct mail: the offer, the list and the creative.

THE OFFER

In my experience the offer is determined by the value of the product on sale. You will not sell a brand-new car or a JCB via direct mail alone without a further stage of face-to-face involvement (although some American whizz-kid has just said that in 10 years' time all cars will be sold via mail order!). You can, however, sell financial products, lower-value consumer products, computer peripherals, and many other items in this way. You must be aware, however, that direct mail is not a 'bandage' – it won't rescue an unrescuable situation. Your product must be at the right price, offered to the right people, totally credible in its presentation, and preferably from a recognized brand or company. Unknown products and brands can work, but it can be that much more difficult.

Case Study

Cable London

Objective:

To help generate enquiries and sales in this highly lucrative market.

Challenge:

This is a highly competitive, price-driven marketplace.

Target market:

'Telephone equipment buyers' in small to medium businesses.

Benefit:

Businesses would receive their telephony at a lower cost than from BT.

Creative platform:

In order to overcome general inertia of BT business customers, we had to devise a campaign that would stand out from the crowd and encourage interaction from the recipient. We produced a mailing around a 'stress reliever' in the shape of a telephone, and sent it in a box along with a questionnaire. The purpose of the questionnaire was to both assess recipients' telephone needs and encourage them to start thinking and questioning their current supplier. Each recipient who sent back a completed questionnaire entered a free prize draw to win a 'telephone chair' for their reception.

Channels/Media:

Direct mail.

Results:

Successful.

It is also vital to make the offer clear and simple; use the KISS – 'Keep It Simple, Stupid' – formula. Most direct mail fails either because the offer is not wanted – your customers of insurance will not automatically want to buy carpets from you – or because the communication is confused and obscure, and doesn't make it clear what the proposition is and what reaction is required from the recipient.

THE LIST

The key to successful direct mail, the list is twice as important as the creative. There are many good lists around and you can usually find the list you want, if you have a highly targeted proposition. If you have a mass-market proposition it can be more difficult, and list testing will be more critical. Lists in the UK fall into four major categories: 'Compiled' and 'Response', which are for business-to-business and consumer, and 'Lifestyle' and 'Voters', which are consumer-only.

Having identified your list, a great deal of detail is required to get it in the format you want and use it in the way you want: recency, frequency, rental, merge/purge, de-duplication, 'nixies', goneaways, mag tape default salutations, and so on. All will be revealed.

THE CREATIVE

This subject merits a book on its own, but basically you must remember that you are writing to people. If you put a brochure in an envelope, you are not using direct mail. There are basic elements in a direct mail pack – envelope, letter, brochure, booster, response mechanism – with as many alternatives as there are standards. What is standard, though, and absolutely immutable, is that you need the following:

- ❏ an outer carrier, in other words an envelope;
- ❏ a response mechanism, such as a card, order form, return envelope, or a telephone number; and
- ❏ marketing material, which includes a letter.

Case Study

Schuler Wine

Product:

Mail-order wines from a Swiss company.

Objectives:

To enter the UK market.

Challenges:

To generate one-stage orders to an unknown supplier.

Target market:

Adult wine buyers.

Offer:

Discounted price and competition to win a holiday.

Creative platform:

Good product presentation coupled with the use of tricks such as calling the order form a 'tasting voucher'.

Channels/Media:

Cold lists of known wine buyers.

Results:

Good.

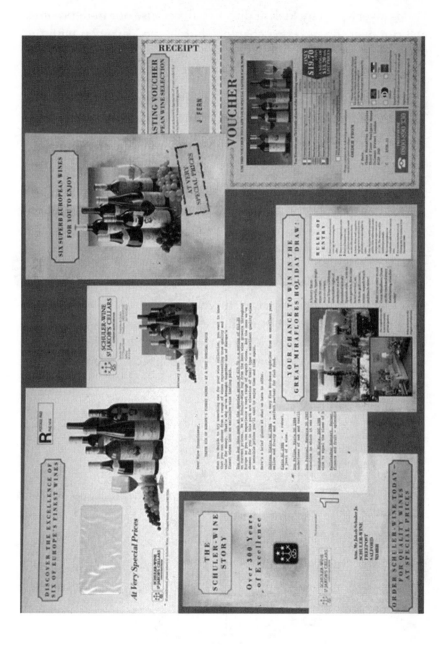

This is a very sketchy look at direct mail, because our in-depth look will run over the next few chapters, but let me leave you with the following thoughts:

1. Direct mail is not a licence to print money.
2. For every seven companies that can use direct mail successfully, three cannot.
3. The traditionally low response levels do not mean that it is not a profitable response medium.
4. Everybody will tell you that direct mail means Reader's Digest and that they hate it and place it in the bin. Ignore them. Reader's Digest are brilliant exponents of direct mail.
5. The hue and cry in the press about junk mail doesn't mean it won't work for you – as long as you get your planning right.
6. If people don't react to your direct mail, you have not offended them by writing to them. They simply place it in the bin in the same way that they turn the page of a newspaper if they do not want to read an advertisement.

5

Understanding the list jungle

The next few chapters will concentrate on lists and the list market, and look in detail at consumer and industrial lists, warm lists and cold lists. At this point we will take an overview of the list market and discuss how you can get the best out of it. This means that we are considering cold lists, because we are talking about the lists you do not have in-house, and that you have to find (warm lists, on the other hand, are usually your own in-house lists of customers and prospects). In order to do this, you will be talking to a list house or a list broker.

These are companies that specialize in the supply of lists for the direct mail market. Some are 'list owners', who have originated the list, by research, advertising or through other methods, and own it. In other cases, 'list managers' have an agreement with a list owner to market that company's list. Lastly, 'list brokers' can arrange to supply you with the appropriate list you are looking for, either from their own 'stable' or from somebody else's. Most list houses fulfil all three functions and the reputable ones belong to the DMA.

Case Study

Cable London

Product:

Major telephony equipment.

Objectives:

To sell latest-generation switchgear into major London companies.

Challenge:

We knew the companies, but we didn't know the individuals who would buy within those companies.

Target market:

Major London companies.

Offer:

If you buy this equipment, you need to talk to us.

Creative platform:

Mailing addressed to 'The Telecommunication Equipment Buyer' on the basis that the mailroom would know who that was, even if we didn't.

Channels/Media:

Cold direct mail.

Results:

Good.

When I asked the major list houses for their ideas and tips on using a list house effectively, they came up with the following golden rules:

1. Take your list broker into your confidence. You cannot expect the best recommendations if you don't give the list house the full brief. Equally, you cannot plan effective roll-outs if you don't share your results. For all you know, an unusual list that worked but which you are discounting could 'ring bells' with the list house in terms of other suitable lists.
2. Be clear about whom you are trying to reach and the objective of your mailing. Again, lateral solutions can emerge if the list house understands what you are trying to achieve.
3. If you have a very tightly defined target market and you are selling a high-value product to, for example, 'personnel managers of timber importers in Scotland', it may pay you to have your list built. It will cost less than mailing all personnel managers in Scotland and there is no point in wasting money on 'mishits'.
4. Use your list broker like your agency. Encourage a proactive relationship and let them provide input to your strategic thinking.
5. Don't rush it and don't leave your list as the last thing to be ordered. It requires as much planning as your creative.
6. Try the unusual. If you have a list that indicates a willingness to purchase through the post, it could work for a wide variety of propositions. One company sold credit card subscriptions successfully to purchasers of muscle-building equipment.
7. Ensure that the list comes with warranties, so that you are complying with the Data Protection Act and other legislation.
8. Establish the ultimate list owner, just to make sure there are no problems.

9. Be clear about the selections you want when you place your order – title, default salutation, output, format, other criteria – but don't just go for a 1 in nth selection (for example, 1 in 10) if there are more selectable criteria available.

10. If you are writing to a very up-market list, check your salutations and titles. It rather upsets members of the House of Lords if they are addressed as Mr. Equally, abbreviated files cause trouble – a recent mailing sent to Arch Cant, Lambeth Palace, and addressed 'Dear Arch' raised a few eyebrows.

11. Check a sample of the list yourself. If you know your market, you'll know if it looks right.

12. Don't abuse your list house. They work on a small commission basis. A list rental of 5,000 just about pays for the phone call they make to you – if you want something complicated, offer to pay for it. It will be worth it in the long term.

"TRUSS $\int$T IN ME"

Case Study

Norwich Union Direct

Product:

Car insurance.

Background:

In 1995, Norwich Union Direct launched car insurance direct to the public via the telephone. During its first two years, a banker pack for new customer acquisition was developed.

Objective:

To improve cost per quotation.

Challenge:

To design a new pack to beat the banker pack.

Target market:

Car owners who had supplied their insurance renewal date to a lifestyle survey.

Offer:

Free insurance quote.

Creative platform:

The issue was to fight the clutter of competitive mailings. The solution was an outer envelope which looked semi-official on manila stock.

Channels/Media:

Direct mail.

Results:

It has consistently generated an outstanding uplift in quotation requests of over 30 per cent.

CREATIVE TARGETING

Can't find the right list? Don't worry! Build your own laterally. In India, a list was created by gathering the names of people queueing at the US Embassy for visas, because they were clearly rich travellers. Get the idea?

If you don't know who buys in a company, just address your mailing to 'The Potato Buyer' or 'The Computer Systems Expert'. There is no law saying you can't make up a job title.

6

Consumer lists

A consumer list is a list of people at their home addresses who would be responsive to a proposition as private individuals, not in their working capacity. When it comes to finding the right cold consumer lists, the problem is less a question of availability than of selection, because there are so many around.

Consumer lists can be categorized in a number of ways. I define four key sections:

- [ ] enquirers;
- [ ] purchasers;
- [ ] residents;
- [ ] lifestyle.

ENQUIRER LISTS

Enquirers, not surprisingly, can give you some of the larger lists in the marketplace – the 20,000s through to the 200,000s. This is because, by definition, many more people will make enquiries about a product than will end up buying it – particularly if the method of enquiry is made easy by Freepost, Freephone, and so on. The nub of the problem with enquirer lists is that you cannot be sure that they will buy your product. More importantly, you do not know whether or not they have 'a propensity to purchase through the post'.

In the UK, one in two adults have purchased through the post in the last 12 months; funnily enough, the figure is identical in the United States. The statistics change slightly if the definition of 'purchase' is widened, to include magazine subscriptions and financial services, for example, but the fact is that a section of the population will never purchase via the post, even though they might express an interest.

Enquirer lists can have merit because they are so diverse. There are lists of enquirers for mail order catalogues, for financial newsletters, for holiday brochures, for car insurance, and so on. You should be able to achieve some marriage of your proposition with the subject of their original interest.

You must establish as much information as you can about such a list – in particular, how old it is, and how aggressively it was followed up by the advertiser. It would also be interesting to know where the enquirers came from; the media alone might tell you whether it is right or wrong for you. I would always recommend as well that you split-run-test an enquirer list against a purchaser list, and don't bother with an enquirer list if you can find the right purchaser list.

Case Study

NDCS

Product:

Charity for deaf children.

Background:

The National Deaf Children's Society raises funds to help deaf children, using proven direct-marketing techniques. Its current pack was tired, and it was looking for a new control.

Objectives:

To increase the response and donation level to the charity from cold lists. To test 'new' pack against present NDCS control pack.

Challenge:

To generate an emotional response to a situation most donors do not relate to.

Target market:

ABC1, over 50 years of age.

Offer:

Please give.

Creative platform:

Very difficult to show deafness, so an earless girl was used to depict the problem. To differentiate from other charity mailers and increase response the copy was rewritten, making it stronger and more emotive than previously. A hard-hitting solution to a difficult creative challenge.

Channels/Media:

Direct mail.

Results:

The 'new' pack beat previous response of control pack by 50 per cent.

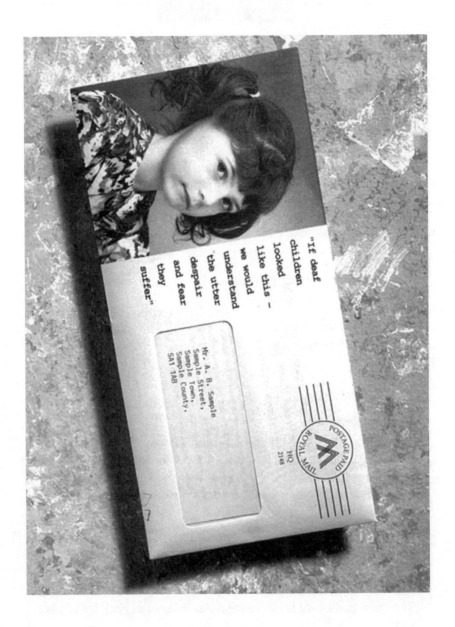

Mr. A. B. Sample
Sample Street,
Sample Town,
Sample County.
SA1 1AB

with the message: "If deaf children looked like this – we would understand the utter despair and fear they suffer"

PURCHASER LISTS

Purchaser lists are obviously spot on, if they are available. Many are not on the market, and those that are have caveats. For example, the Franklin Mint won't rent you its list if you want to sell limited-edition collectable china, but there are many correlations that do work – china to purchasers of fine wine, fundraising catalogues to mail order customers, garden equipment to seed purchasers. The key tips to watch for are value and sex. If you have a list of people who have purchased low-value items, in whatever field, they are less likely to purchase high-value items from you. If you want to sell to men, you need to find lists of male purchasers (unless you believe your product can be bought as a present by the wife, but that could give timing problems).

Again, you need to know the age of the list and whether it's been rented recently. If it is regularly used, so much the better. Payment methods could be important as well. If you want credit card sales, it's no good using a list where the average order value is £5 and payments were not by credit card. Allowing for these restrictions, purchaser lists are by and large well worth having. You can afford to be a bit lateral as well in how you select. If you cannot find an exact match, don't despair. For example, if you want to sell souvenirs of Britain's industrial past, why not try a list of people who have taken weekend breaks in Britain in places of industrial heritage? If you want to sell tennis courts, why not try owners of swimming pools – or vice versa?

RESIDENT LISTS

The next consumer list is the electoral roll, which is why I call it the resident list. It is up to date, accurate and incredibly powerful at a local level. Indeed, if you want to do a local consumer mailing, or mail to specific parts of a region, this is likely to be the only relevant list. As it is updated every year, it is accurate and it can also be segmented by type of household, for example family, single man, single woman.

It also has what is called the 'B' list – house movers – as well as young people as they become eligible to vote, and it can also be beneficial for mailing the neighbours of your customers. Naturally, it's fully postcoded, so geographically it is very accurate, but of course it says nothing about who people are and what they are likely to buy. That is where profiling systems come into play; we'll look at them next.

LIFESTYLE LISTS

Finally, lifestyle lists contain millions of names culled from shoppers' questionnaires, where numerous questions are asked about which brands are purchased and about the hobbies, interests and lifestyles of the respondents. Such lists are very powerful where there is an interest or lifestyle match with your product, and they are responsive by definition.

Leeds Visa

Product:

Affinity Visa Card.

Background:

This was the UK's first affinity card. After being sold in to the house file, this was the first move into cold lists.

Objective:

To recruit new cardholders.

Challenge:

This campaign was mounted before it was common to sell credit cards via direct mail.

Target market:

Creditworthy B, C1, C2 households.

Offer:

The card that helps your choice of charities.

Creative platform:

The card was the hero so we made it dominate the pack.

Channels/Media:

Direct-mail pack mailed to a cold list from the NDL Lifestyle Selector. The pack was split run against the control pack. Imaginative creative solution of a giant-sized card.

Results:

Target response index: 100; actual response index: 300.

In conclusion, good consumer lists give you purchasing tips and hints, and named individuals. Whatever you want to sell, you should be able to find the right cold list.

7

Yuppies, Dinkys, et al

We all love categorizing people, don't we? Yuppies drive Porsches, Dinkys have no kids. Well, in direct marketing, we have an actual science based on categorization, called 'profiling'. The grand-daddy of profiling systems in the UK is ACORN. It is worth explaining its history in detail, as it sheds light on the principles of profiling.

ACORN was developed as a concept by Richard Webber when he was working for the Centre for Environmental Studies. The aim was to identify areas of stress and deprivation in inner cities for extra grant funding, but it was quickly recognized that such a concept also identified areas of high consumer spending power. ACORN was launched commercially by CACI in 1977.

The fundamental thinking behind ACORN, and indeed behind all the other profiling systems, is that 'birds of a feather flock together'. In other words, if you have a good customer in Acacia Road, Bristol, the chances are that the other people in Acacia Road would also be good customers; and if it were possible to find other locations in the country where area, housing and lifestyle were similar to those of Acacia Road, you would be likely to find good customers there too. The principle is reflected in the name ACORN, which is an acronym that stands for 'A Classification Of Residential Neighbourhoods'.

ACORN is based on the 10-yearly census data released by OPCS (the Office of Population and Census Statistics) at Enumeration District (ED) level – in other words, the districts into which the UK is divided for the purposes of taking the census. This ensures the confidentiality that is guaranteed under law in respect of every person's individual census form.

At ED level a certain amount of data – 40 sets in total, known as 'variables' – is identified as being relevant for marketing purposes. These variables fall into three distinct categories: demographic, socio-economic and housing. For each ED we know, for example, the percentage penetration of young people with families, senior managers and white collar workers, and houses with more than seven rooms.

For ACORN, these 40 variables were clustered together using iterative relocation. Basically, these clever words mean that each ED has a recognizable pattern across the 40 variables, and that a computer identifies where each pattern is replicated in another ED. Out of the computer process, each ED was assigned to a previously identified ED pattern, or a new one was created. At the end of the exercise, the whole country had been 'patterned' into 38 neighbourhood types.

S.N.A.G. 'SENSITIVE NEW AGE GUY'

Case Study

Norton Strawberries

Product:

Pick your own strawberries.

Objective:

To drive to the fields customers who would buy large quantities for jam and other cooking, rather than customers who 'ate' in the field and bought one punnet.

Challenge:

To communicate only with those sectors of the community who are in the right target market.

Target market:

High-value pickers.

Offer:

Free recipe and free strawberries.

Creative platform:

Very strawberry.

Channels/Media:

Profiled (ACORN) door-to-door was used.

Results:

Doubled sales compared with local newspaper advertising.

The types were organized into 11 neighbourhood groups, which were given A–K alpha codes. For example, Group A was Agricultural Areas and its two types were farmers and farm workers. Group B was Barratt-land and the types covered the spectrum from first-time owner-occupier semis or maisonettes to big, posh detacheds in cul-de-sacs. The 38 types tell us, therefore, about the housing and the people in the housing.

It's important to bear in mind that it's not a perfect system – no system ever is – because the Government controls the boundaries of the EDs. It could be possible to get one that's half-council and half-private, or one where 75 per cent are young families and 25 per cent are OAPs, which is difficult for marketing purposes. However, the probabilities are good, and the ACORN principle represented a revolution when it burst on the market.

Each ED was cross-tabulated with the postcodes that fell wholly or mainly within the ED. Therefore, it was possible to look at any of the 1.3 million postcodes in the UK and know its ACORN type – young, old, up-market, down-market, and so on. And it's that postcode link that makes ACORN and the other systems a practical profile of customers and purchasers.

Profiles are obtained in one of two ways. The ideal is to profile a customer name and address list whereby the ACORN type of each address is identified, and then the numbers in each are compared with the country (or region, or other specified area) as a whole to establish under- or over-penetration. For example, a manufacturer of water beds may have an index of 300 on K37 – areas of prosperous retired pensioners. That means, in percentage terms, three times as many K37s on file as in the country as a whole, and gives a strong segment to go after.

Case Study

Schreiber Kitchens

Product:

New kitchens.

Objective:

To generate traffic into Schreiber showrooms.

Challenge:

To target likely households and motivate them to visit.

Target market:

Homeowners in the catchment area of the showrooms.

Offer:

Free book for visit.

Creative platform:

Personalized, individual 'invitation'.

Channels/Media:

ACORN-profiled electoral roll.

Results:

4 to 1 ROI.

For people who do not have a name and address file, there are published research surveys called 'omnibus', such as Target Group Index and National Readership Survey, where ACORN codes have been allocated to the addresses of all the people who took part in the survey. Thus we know the ACORN profile of people who take holidays abroad, for example, or who read *The Guardian*.

ACORN and other profiling systems make the electoral roll work as a cold mailing list, because it is possible to pick off the names and addresses in the ACORN types you want. So, for example, the water bed manufacturer would rent from the electoral roll names and addresses in Type 37 in, say, Bournemouth.

Since ACORN, a number of competitors have appeared on the market, all working on fundamentally the same principle. MOSAIC from Experian has extra information, particularly financial, within its database over and above the census. CAMEO UK is also census-based, but was also the first to be Windows-based and is very user-friendly.

8

Business lists

Let us move now from consumer lists to business lists, a major jungle in their own right. In my opinion there are two major problems when working with business lists. The first is the lack of the right name of an individual to whom to write. The second is the poor segmentation available to identify exactly who your buyers are likely to be.

Many business lists do not come with named individuals and, to be honest, it can be better to write to a job title, such as 'The Managing Director'. That way, at least your mailing should land on the right desk, even if it is not personalized. Some lists do carry named individuals but you have to be very sure that the list is clean, or you run the risk of your mailing actually following an individual to another company in an entirely different line of business.

Case Study

Trade Indemnity

Product:

Credit insurance.

Objective:

To generate leads for the sales force.

Challenge:

Trade indemnity is a very complex product, and usually a distress purchase.

Target market:

Credit managers and financial directors.

Creative platform:

Two mailing packs, one a questionnaire, were tested against an insert. The creative imagery was clear, with graphic representation of what may be lost by those without credit insurance.

Channels/Media:

A fully integrated campaign comprising inserts placed in a range of business titles, and a direct mailing to the target audience at their business address.

Results:

	Target index	Actual index
Direct mail	100	125
Inserts	100	122

Questionnaire out-pulled image pack.

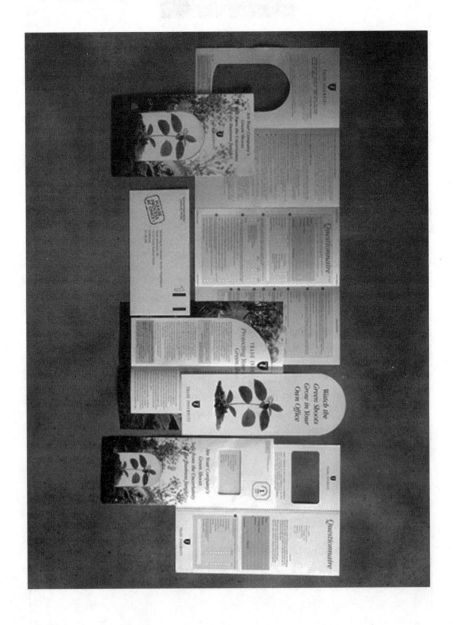

The segmentation can also be singularly lacking. If you wish to reach a highly defined segment – the construction industry, timber importers, or whatever – there will probably be a good list. However, if you want to sell something broad-based, such as computers or cars, it is virtually impossible to identify which companies would be in the market for such products, which are most likely to purchase, and who the decision-maker is.

In addition, regionality is very difficult. Many lists are so small nationally that the minimum rental quantity makes it impossible to take, for example, Yorkshire only. Those lists that are large enough to split geographically tend to be bland and untargeted.

So what sort of business lists do exist? The first category are directories, where lists have been compiled from major directories, such as Kompass. This effectively gives you an all-UK database where the type of industry should be very accurate. There are usually no named individuals, though, and, given the lead times for compiling these directories, quite often size, turnover and even location can be wrong.

The second type of list is made up of exhibition attendees, created from the information cards completed by visitors at trade fairs and exhibitions. Obviously, such lists have named individuals and up-to-date information, although it can deteriorate quickly. However, a mixed calibre of people come to any exhibition; visitors to a computer exhibition, for example, are not necessarily looking to buy a computer. They could be competitive suppliers, or junior members of staff sent to learn.

The third type of lists are publishers' lists, made up of people who subscribe to trade and technical publications which they receive through the post. These lists tend to be accurate and clean, with named individuals, but you obviously have to have the right magazine in the first place. Trade magazines are either 'vertical' or 'horizontal' in their readership. If you want to reach accountants and others in chemical engineering you need a vertical publication, in other words one that goes to the chemical engineering industry only. If you want to reach accountants in a variety of industries, you use a horizontal accountancy publication, which goes to accountants working across many industries.

There are other sorts of business lists on the market, gathered from a variety of sources. Some are good, some are not. One or two list houses have also built their own business databases, and take the responsibility for keeping them clean, ie up to date. To get a good business list, the only advice I can really offer is go for the cleanest and most tightly defined, and look for an identified 'responsive' individual. If in doubt, don't do it.

Case Study

Newsweek

Objectives:

To increase subscriptions to *Newsweek*.

Challenge:

To beat the control pack used for recruitment, which had been unbeatable for four years.

Target market:

Senior professionals and business people.

Offers:

Limited trial period before payment. Discounted subscription in rising tiers, depending on length of subscription. Up to 65 per cent discount for a two-year subscription. A free gift of a personal organizer on payment of subscription.

Creative platform:

The strategy was to knowingly break business-to-business direct-marketing rules by making the mailing to business people look like a down-market consumer catalogue mailing. The personalization, the scratch-and-reveal mystery gift, the offer stickers and the poly envelope were all a deliberate attempt to play to the little child inside every business person.

Channels/Media:

A combination of 10 lifestyle, compiled, subscription and response lists which had previously been tested by the client was used. This exercise was a creative test, not a list test.

Results:

Response rate 10.4 per cent higher than the control. Average subscription term increased by 45 per cent compared with the control.

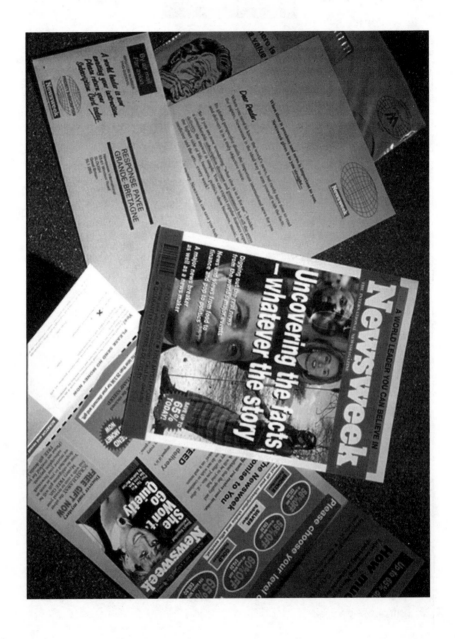

LIST-RENTING RULES

When it comes to renting a list, whether consumer or business, bear in mind the following points:

1. Rent or buy? Most lists are available for rental only but a few are for sale. I would rarely advise anyone to buy because you must test the list to see if it is any good and, if you buy it, it is up to you to keep it clean. This is a major task usually undertaken by the list owner. Remember, when you rent a list you are paying for one-time rental only. Do not re-use the list without paying for it. You will be found out, because all list owners put sleeper names (known as 'seed' names) in their lists, which you will not be able to identify.

2. Minimum rental. All lists have minimum rental quantities which you must allow for in your budgeting. With most business lists it is 3,000, with most consumer lists 5,000 and with the electoral roll 10,000.

3. Recency. You must ask when the list was most recently rented. If it has not been used for quite a while that could be bad news. It usually means the list industry won't use it because they know it's no good.

4. Frequency. You must also ask how frequently the list has been used in the last year. Frequent usage means it's a good list that works. There is the famous story from the United States of the mail order company which split its list in half, and put half out on the open list market. At the end of 12 months it compared the sales of its own goods via the section of the file that hadn't been rented to third parties with sales made via the section that had been rented. Those on the half of the list that had been rented had spent more money with the list owner! Regular usage keeps a list fresh.

5. Format. You need to know the format in which you want to take the list. Do you want self-adhesive labels, a magnetic tape, a CD-ROM or just a listing for data re-capture?
6. Selection. All lists have selection criteria. Do you want a selection by Mr or Mrs, or by job title, by geography, or by turnover of company, or number of employees? Such selections usually cost more.
7. Net names. Suppose you have 5,000 dentists who are customers and there are 10,000 dentists you don't trade with. If you want to test part of a dentist list you don't want to write to existing customers, so you would do a merge/purge. Most list owners would then rebate you the rental costs on the duplication established up to about 85 per cent. This is known as a net name deal.
8. 'Nixies' or 'goneaways'. With any mailing you will get returns 'not known at this address'. Keep them and pass them back to the list house so the list can be cleaned. If you get more than 5 per cent returns, you have the basis of renegotiating the rental charge.

9

A picture is worth a thousand words – not!

Well, actually, in direct mail a picture isn't worth a thousand words. Experience has shown that copy is far more important in direct mail than visuals. So, the golden rule is 'start with the words'.

This chapter will concentrate in particular on creativity for direct mail. There are as many creative solutions as there are clients and products – as I'm sure you know, from receiving mail yourself – but this is a basics book, so let's stick to the standard rules that should make the difference between success and failure.

CORPORATE AND BRAND POSITIONING

Believe it or not, this is a key part of the success of direct mail. You and your products/services must look credible and authoritative. If you have a nationally known name, fine. If not, be sure that you are using the best possible name and positioning. So it's not just what you call yourself, but how you show that visually in terms of logo, graphics, and so on.

Assuming you've got all that right, let's look at the contents of a mailing pack.

Case Study

BP

Product:

Diesel oil for lorry drivers.

Objective:

To restimulate lorry drivers back into promotional scheme.

Challenge:

To attract attention of lorry drivers.

Target market:

Lorry drivers registered in promotional scheme.

Offer:

Great new prizes now available.

Creative platform:

Envelope designed around lorry illustration.

Channels/Media:

In-house file.

Results:

Good.

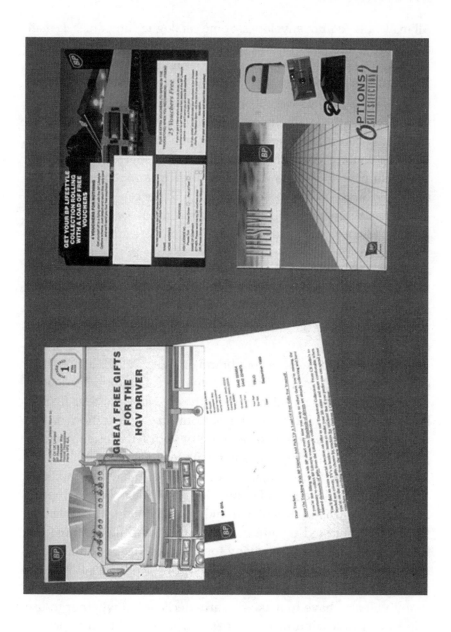

ENVELOPES

All mailshots require envelopes. Some catalogue companies *do* mail out without an envelope, but behaviourally we expect to open an envelope, and I would always use one. Polythene can be used as an alternative to paper envelopes, but is mainly used for weight saving if a mailing is near its weight limit, or for cost saving on very large runs. Never use polythene on fewer than 100,000, unless weight dictates. If you do find yourself using polythene, look carefully at whether you are going to buy pre-made envelopes which require hand filling, or flat rolls for machine wrapping; and remember, polythene can depress your response by up to 20 per cent.

As far as messages on envelopes are concerned, my advice is to use them. My experience is that they uplift response – and I have tested them many times. Make sure your message is interesting and relevant. Never use a message like 'private and confidential' or 'important documents enclosed' to 'con' your reader. You will only create feelings of disappointment when the mailing is opened if you do. You may also be answerable to the Advertising Standards Authority.

In addition, don't expose your brand on the envelope unless it is a customer mailing, or your brand is so powerful that it will enhance the envelope message. I always write the envelope message first, as it clarifies my thinking on the bottom-line proposition of the mailing, and indeed the first sentence of your letter often makes a good envelope line when you end it with leader dots (. . .).

Unless your mailing is small enough for you to hand-stamp, look at having a PPI (Postage Paid Impression) printed on the envelope. It is much neater than Royal Mail franking, and avoids the problem of some being franked upside down, thus obscuring the message. Remember that if you are paying for PPI printing, your marketing message is printed free. Also, always print a return address for 'goneaways' – it makes you more popular with the Royal Mail.

You will also have to make an early decision on whether to use window or non-window envelopes. If you are using any form of personalization, a window makes sense, as it saves the cost of reproducing the address twice. It also gives you the opportunity of having your address carrier double as your response device if you want to keep 'trace codes' with the name and address. Trace codes are alpha or numeric codes put on the reply piece for the purpose of quickly working out where the response has come from: which list it is from, which offer etc.

You can, of course, use self-adhesive labels as an alternative and put them on the envelope. This is certainly the cheapest if you are on a tight budget, but self-adhesive labels do need to be fixed by hand.

The size of envelope you use is also a key decision – the larger, the more expensive. The three standard sizes normally used in direct mail are DL (holds A4 folded into thirds), C5 (holds A5 paper and A4 folded once), and C4 (holds A4 paper). Many mailings are quite satisfactory at DL size, but you need larger if you have a larger brochure. Obviously, C4 is the most expensive, but it can create higher response because it has greater impact.

Case Study

Beneficial Bank plc

Product:

Visa card designed for the charity Donor 2000.

Objectives:

To open new Visa accounts, and to increase the number of donor card holders.

Challenge:

A multi-layered message. It's a credit card plus a charity support plus the proof of registering for organ donation, plus the card for emergencies.

Target market:

Registered organ donors, and members of the general public who had visited the field-force stand at motorway services.

Offers:

No annual fee, low rates and donation to charity for card account opening and usage.

Creative platform:

An impactful outer envelope introduced the theme of testimonials from recipients of donor organs. The strong emotional messages were supplemented by key product benefits (no fee, low rate), to form a convincing proposition.

Channels/Media:

Direct mail. The mailing was timed to coincide with a national awareness campaign for donor cards. Test card recruitment to cold prospects through a hired field force positioned at locations such as motorway service areas.

Results:

33 per cent above target.

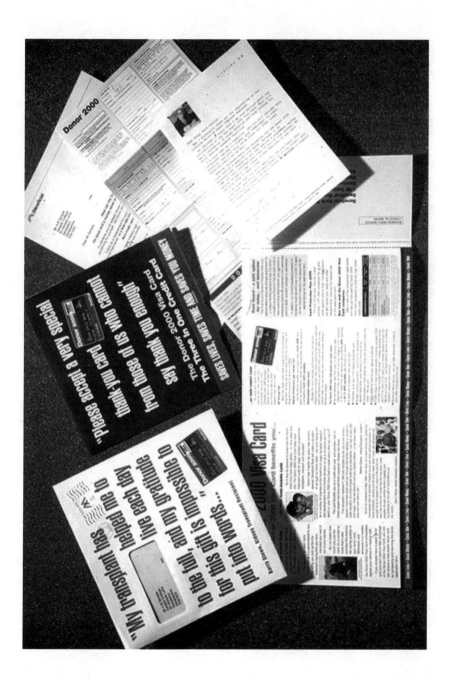

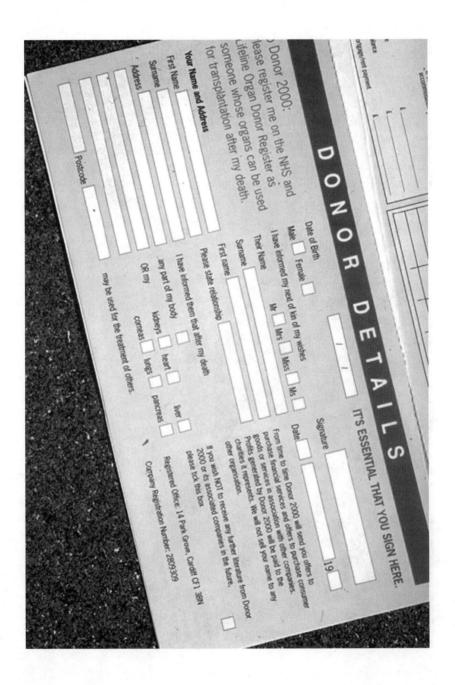

LETTERS

The single most important element in a direct mail pack is the letter. Whatever else you omit, don't leave out the letter. People expect to receive one when they open a mailing and it is the first element they will read. There is endless debate about how long direct mail letters should be. The simple answer is: as long as it needs to be! Don't pad them and don't cram them, but do remember that the letter is a substitute salesman – it's you talking to your prospects. It won't do to be very brief and terse: 'I thought you might like to know about our amazing new product, so I've enclosed a brochure.' The letter must always work as a stand-alone, so it must cover all the points in detail.

The starting point should be the headline, which encapsulates the message and may be very similar to that on the envelope. The headline may be typed across the top of the letter below the salutation or typeset in large size in the top right-hand corner, or even put in a Johnson box – bang in the middle at the top of the page and surrounded by asterisks.

You must then move into the first paragraph, which should come straight out with the benefits of what you are selling. Don't expect people to plough through several paragraphs of verbosity to get to the core of your message. When writing the letter, remember the golden rule of 'short words, short sentences, short paragraphs'. You're not trying to get an MA in English!

Avoid the 'we-we' factor at all costs. Use the word 'you' wherever you can. After all, the recipient is not interested in who you are or what you do, but in what your product or service can do for him. Believe it yourself and write it convincingly. Put in lots of benefits, and be absolutely clear about what you are offering and what response is required. It often helps, after you have written your first draft, to discard the first sentence or even the first paragraph. We frequently take too much time to get to the point!

Give your letter some 'air' with indented paragraphs and plenty of space so that it looks easy to read. Underline judiciously to bring out key points. Always have a PS to push the key message (free gift, special offer), as the PS will always be read – and usually first. If your letter uses more than one side, break copy in mid-sentence so that the reader continues to read.

Keep the type size reasonable, unless you're selling to teenagers. One in two people over the age of 45 wear glasses, and we struggle with small type! However, people do enjoy and read handwritten margin notes and other 'bits' with handwriting.

10

A picture is worth a thousand words – maybe!

Let's go on to the brochure. It would be very rare for a mailshot not to carry a brochure, which functions as product literature. Your existing literature may do the job, but usually you need to create something new. There are two reasons for this: size and message. Many mailings will work at C5 or DL size, but many brochures are produced at A4 size, hence the need to redesign for size or cost.

Secondly, you need continuity of message from your envelope and letter into your literature. It doesn't help if your envelope and letter talk about 'the cheapest possible home contents insurance', and the brochure talks about 'a policy that automatically includes swimming pools or greenhouses', for example.

Whether or not you produce the literature in full colour will probably be dictated by your product and your size. Expensive products from well-established companies need full colour to maintain corporate position; fashion products need full colour for a total sell; but widgets, nuts and bolts and many services would work in two colours.

Case Study

NatWest

Product:

Card Plus account, a bank account designed for 13- to 20-year-olds.

Objective:

To persuade savings account customers to open a Card Plus account.

Challenges:

1. Strong competition from other banks aiming at young adults.
2. Designing a communication that would appeal to the target age group while working within set corporate image guidelines of NatWest.

Target market:

Existing customers with a First Reserve savings account, aged 13–16.

Offer:

£20 money-off voucher from HMV and 12 'buy one, get one free' Pizza Hut vouchers, plus either £10 HMV voucher or four free pizzas from Pizza Hut.

Creative platform:

The distinctive square mailing featured brightly coloured Lichtenstein-style comic-strip illustrations, which were directly relevant to the target audience. The offer was emphasized with strong pictorial references and the product benefits were given in a clear, impactful way through simple, 'youth-style' copy. Basically, we wanted to talk to these young adults in a manner which they could relate to and understand.

Results:

Exceeded target by 122 per cent!

A picture is worth a thousand words – maybe!

BOOSTER

The booster is so-called because its objective is to boost response, and it can contain a wide variety of messages. One of the most common purposes is to feature in more detail a free gift, incentive, prize draw or competition. Here you can show photographs or illustrations of free gifts, and use more copy to explain the attractiveness of the freebie. Other functions of a booster can include rebuttal of negatives – 'if you do not want our catalogue, please read this anyway' – repayment/calculation tables, or question and answer copy explaining the more complex points of the proposition.

LIFT LETTER

This is a second letter from a different person, sometimes the MD, sometimes a satisfied customer. It is always physically smaller than the main letter and is usually produced in a script typeface.

OTHER MATERIAL

The possibilities are endless – extra product information, more promotional items and so on. The golden rule though is 'logical'; every piece of paper should be in the mailing for a reason, and that reason should be clear to the recipient.

RESPONSE MECHANISM

This is vital. You are engaged in direct mail to generate response, not to make you feel better. The key here is to be absolutely clear about the response you require. If it involves one stage – generating an order – then at the very least you need a reply envelope. This should be first class Business Reply, to express urgency; it can even have 'priority' or other urgent messages printed on it. Even if you are looking for responses over the phone or on the Internet, you should still have the hard-copy option, for comfort, familiarity, and 'pattern' recognition.

Sophisticated users of direct mail often prefer 'bangtail' envelopes, with a large flap that can be torn off which can carry additional offers or 'recommend-a-friend' devices, for example. These are only cost-effective in larger runs.

To support the reply envelope, you need the paperwork to go in it; make it easy for people to react. If you are selling, this is an order form, of which there are two kinds: 'self-completion' and 'laundry list'.

Self-completion expects the customer to write in the articles being ordered and tends to have between six and eleven lines for placing an order. (To increase average order value, many companies put in a 'golden line' promotion, for example pre-printing on the sixth or seventh line, offering a free gift only given if the number of lines entered reaches the 'golden line'.)

Laundry lists are particularly powerful in the catalogue market for uplifting sales. They work on the principle of listing every item in the catalogue, so that the customer only has to complete the 'quantity' and 'total' boxes. (This is feasible up to about 500 lines.)

The key point with order forms is good art direction. They must be very clear and simple to complete, with a number of selling messages: 'Complete and Return Today', 'Take Advantage of the Special Offer Now!', and so on.

For a two-stage response, it is usual to use a reply paid card, as this is the most convenient. Provided people are only asking for more information, and not revealing any confidential details, a card is fine. With a card it is always sensible to include a number of tick boxes, as this turns it into an involvement device. For example, 'Please send me details of your widgets. I am particularly interested in red ones, blue ones, left-handed ones, right-handed ones, other. Please specify'.

Case Study

OAG Reed Travel

Product:

Cargo Disk. A new PC-based cargo/freight scheduling product with details of every airline's cargo flight schedules around the world.

Objectives:

1. To launch a new product to the target market.
2. To convert existing, book-based users to PC-based Cargo Disk.
3. To expand the market share of OAG in the USA.
4. To generate qualified leads by encouraging trial of the product.

Target market:

Existing users of OAG paper-based guides in the UK and the USA.

Offer:

A free demo disk of the product as an incentive to respond.

Creative platform:

Basically, our strategy was one of 'toys for the boys'! A free aeroplane in every mail pack.

The copyline 'Around the world in 80 seconds' emphasized the main benefits of the product by conveying the speed and efficiency with which users could access the information.

Channels/Media:

Direct mail to in-house database in the UK and the USA.

Results:

A huge 26 per cent response rate.

'I FEEL NAKED, COULD YOU PUT ADDRESS ON ME?'

Also, give people an opportunity to be more committed – 'Please send your rep in', 'Please contact me to arrange a demonstration' – and always get their telephone numbers in a business-to-business situation. It can also be quite beneficial to ask people to say, 'No. Thank you, but I am not interested'. It helps to clean the list you are using but also, in the consumer market, you can treat the no's as yes's with a fair degree of confidence, as genuine no's don't even respond.

Creatively for direct mail, the key rules are:

1. copy first, visuals second;
2. consistency of message throughout;
3. strong calls to action; and
4. clear, easy response mechanisms.

11

If you touch it, you feel it

Don't even begin to think of direct mail as postal advertising. That it can do, but only with big brands and big budgets. In the world of DIY direct marketing, you need to remember that direct mail is a *tactile* medium. Your recipients touch and feel your direct mail. Touch is vitally important as one of the five senses, and is the one sense that always comes into play in direct mail.

Even on a budget, think about how your direct mail *feels*. Think about the sort of paper you use – coarse, smooth, shiny, dull. Think about your use of colour, of photography, of visuals. Does the feel of the paper reflect the proposition of the visual and copy? Think about your printing techniques. Relatively cheap ideas, such as unusual folds, or die cuts, can make your pack look and feel different.

Case Study

Beneficial Bank

Product:

Unsecured loans.

Objectives:

1. To persuade retail finance customers to take out a personal loan and consolidate their existing retail credit and other credit commitments.
2. To encourage existing loan customers to take out increased lending.
3. To encourage lapsed customers to borrow again.

Challenge:

To overcome the ongoing competitive activity in the personal loans marketplace.

Target market:

The mailing was targeted to existing credit customers who were part way through their repayment term, and lapsed customers.

Offer:

A 'top-up' loan, ie, further credit based on the customers' outstanding debt compared to their credit limit.

Creative platform:

The loan offer was enhanced through the inclusion of a pair of scissors as an involvement device. Customers were encouraged to 'snip their monthly bills'.

Channels/Media:

This mailing formed part of an ongoing monthly mailing campaign.

Results:

This equated to a 25 per cent increase in business over the same period in 1996.

If you really want your pack to stand out, look at what I call '3-D mail', where you use something other than paper. It doesn't need to be expensive. If you sell wine, put a cork in the envelope; if you want to talk about a fresh, new idea, mail an apple. (But don't ever mail confetti – it goes everywhere!) The beauty of all 3-D mail is that it cleverly overrides any negatives of an unsolicited mailshot. If you can feel there is something inside the envelope, or if you receive an intriguing box, you want to open it.

This is also good for getting past secretaries in larger companies who filter their bosses' mail, so it's a particular boon in business-to-business. If you're not feeling creative, why not put in a sample of your product? Even if steel or plastic or packaging is not intrinsically fascinating, a piece of it in a box *can* be, particularly if you make a game around it, like a puzzle.

Case Study

BSkyB

Product:

Sky satellite TV service.

Objectives:

To maximize the number of ex-subscribers responding to reinstate, and maximize retention of these customers after the initial 30-day free offer period.

Challenges:

To create an impactful format and creative hook which was unique and innovative, to differentiate the mailing from other mailings previously received.

Target market:

Lapsed subscribers.

Offer:

The banker offer to this audience was a 30-day free trial so that the ex-subscribers could experience what had changed on Sky since they cancelled their subscriptions.

Creative platform:

This format was designed to maximize the impact of personalization and to carry the offer message in an impactful and familiar tabloid newspaper style. The prospect's name was incorporated into the newspaper editorial in 18 places, using a lasering technique that had never been used before in the UK.

Results:

Target (index) personalized newspaper 100; Actual (index) 184.

THE DAILY SKY

BOOK YOUR SEAT FOR THE BEST 30 DAYS ON THE BOX
CALL NOW ON **0990 10 20 30**
and quote reference number below.
See page 2, col 1 for details

June/July 1997   FREE   THE BEST FOR TV ENTERTAINMENT

Mr Sample saves £££s with no strings attached

By Maude Osh

Financial Correspondent

Sky is prepared to give away 30 days of free Sky TV to Mr Sample in his home today. In a deal that will save £26.99, Mr Sample has not only shown a shrewd financial sense, but also the ability to spot a winner.

A Sky spokesperson has also confirmed that there is absolutely no commitment to carry on, and no strings attached.

Mr Sample should be pleased to know that continuing to subscribe beyond the 30 days FREE offer period is easy. Simply keep viewing and Sky will automatically start your billing. Otherwise simply call on 01506 496500 before the 30 day period is up and we will switch you off.

It was also stressed that although this offer is quick and easy to arrange, the offer must end on June 22nd. A source close to Sky advised that Mr Sample should act right away by calling Sky on **0990 10 20 30.**

SAVE £26.99 TODAY

Daily Sky TV sensation

MR SAMPLE RETURNS:

30 days' FREE Sky

Offer proves irresistible

By Mo Veestar
Showbiz Correspondent

In a renewed bid to bring back one of its most valued former viewers, Sky is ready to give Mr Sample 30 days of FREE Sky TV. All of Sky's channels are being offered absolutely free with no catch, to show just how much sensational new entertainment Mr Sample has been missing.

All Sky channels are free for 30 days, which means Mr Sample can see over 450 movies a month on three movie channels, over 300 hours of sport a week on Sky's three sports channels, plus the fabulous Disney Channel too. A reliable source informs us that Mr Sample has recently been checking the Sky listings from

the comfort of his home. And, if our source is to be believed, Mr Sample will be enjoying the best in home entertainment with films like Casino and Murder In The First, as well as joining the England football team in the exciting pre-World Cup festival, LeTournoi and settling down with the British Lions Rugby Tour to South Africa, shown exclusively live on Sky.

Sky will make it easy to see these forthcoming events by offering all Sky channels FREE for 30 days. All Mr Sample has to do is ...

...Call Sky Now, on 0990 10 20 30.

Mr A B Sample
96A Sample Street Lane
Sample Town
Sample City
Sample County
AB99 ABn

Customer Account Number: PROSPECT99
When calling please quote reference: FH72-JNFN

Movie Exclusive:

Mr Sample comes face to face with *The American President*
on The Movie Channel

Exclusively Live Summer Soccer Special:

Mr Sample joins England in France for a pulsating World Cup warm-up
Le Tournoi: England, Italy, Brazil and France – June 3-11

LE TOURNO — Exclusive Sky Sports spectaculars — See Back Page **BRITISH LIONS**

Remember that direct mail is the only tactile medium, and think about how people will react to the touch of the mailing, the feel of the mailing, the interactivity of the mailing, the participation of the mailing, and the dimensionality of the mailing.

Equally importantly, don't forget how you use personalization. There is only one rule here – get it right! If you misspell my name or address in any way, I will not care how interesting your proposition is. Assuming you can get it right, think about going further than mere salutation. 'Dear Mrs Donovan' is fine, but if my name also appears in the letter text, I will be drawn to the copy. After all, the most powerful icon in the world (after 'free') is one's own name.

If you have a database, use the information: 'Last time you ordered an XXXX'; 'We haven't heard from you since July'. Remember, people don't buy from boring people, so why should they buy from boring mailshots?

Case Study

Telecom Act

Product:

Computer consultancy.

Objective:

To generate leads.

Challenge:

Before the days when outsourcing was normal. So how to communicate the product?

Target market:

IT managers in medium to large companies.

Offer:

We solve your overload headaches.

Creative platform:

Problem visualized with pill bottle containing Smarties.

Channels/Media:

Cold direct mail.

Results:

Excellent.

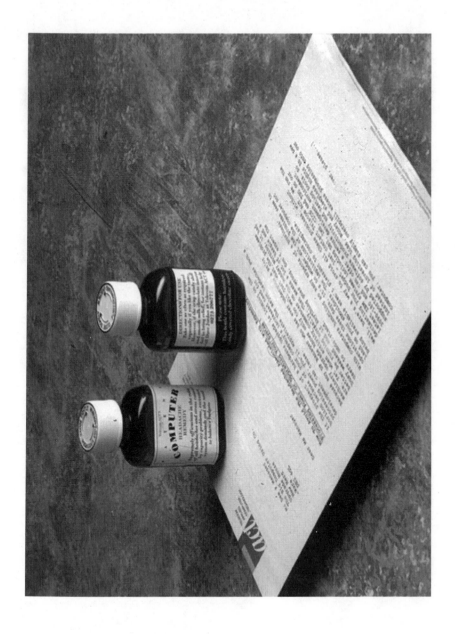

12

From shoe box to computer: what is a database?

The current industry joke is that one name is a name, two names are a list and three names are a database. There's more than a grain of truth in that. For many industries, 'database' is really only a posh word for lists or, rather, what you do with lists when you've got them.

Let us start from a presumption, therefore, that what we are talking about is name and address data and how to exploit it. Why name and address? Because you recoup your investment in a database by being able to maximize your communication opportunities to present, past and future customers. Other statistical information is great fun, but it doesn't pay the mortgage. Getting more from existing customers and getting more customers does that.

To that extent, the shoe box, the filing cabinet, and so on, are all databases, because they store your individual customer and prospect data. However, not only are they clumsy, slow and unwieldy to operate, they are also virtually impossible to cross-tabulate. For example, if you have a list of doctors in a filing cabinet, each card tells you who the doctor is, where they operate, when a rep last visited them, what they buy from you, when they last ordered, and so on. However, imagine the logistical problem of asking your secretary, 'Give me the names of all the doctors who have bought penicillin from us in the last three months where they haven't seen a rep for over six months.' It can't be done manually, but a computer can do it.

'YES! I'VE THREE NAMES – I'VE GOT A DATABASE!'

Case Study

British Fuels

Product:

Coal, coal products and coal-burning accessories such as companion sets, fireguards, etc.

Objectives:

To protect BFL's market share in the domestic coal-burning market. To gain information on fuel usage via a questionnaire.

Challenge:

To generate loyalty in an extremely promiscuous market, ensuring repeat purchase via BFL coal merchants.

Target market:

Coal consumers, mainly traditional working class.

Offer:

Vouchers which could be redeemed for horse brasses or discounts off related coal products were awarded every time recipients purchased coal.

Creative platform:

The copy, tone and imagery were highly relevant to the target market, presenting an aspirational but achievable offer.

Channels/Media:

Lists of existing customers supplied by coal merchants.

Results:

	Target index	Actual index
Questionnaires returned	100	200
Vouchers redeemed	100	300

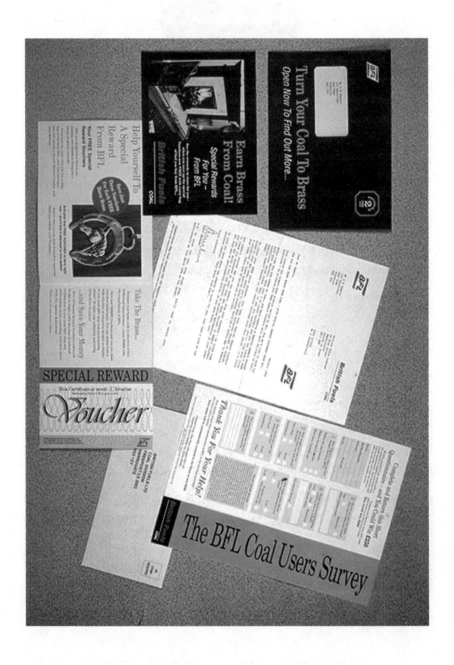

Databases emerged because computers became smaller, more powerful and less expensive, and because the direct-mail industry produced software that would answer its own specific questions. Although you can go some way manually, it's not very easy or very fast. Let us talk, therefore, about building a computer-based resource from scratch. I am not going to talk technically about hardware or software, but about what you need to put in and what you need to get out.

Your starting point is existing customers. You need your database to be driven primarily by them, as they represent real live information that you then supplement. Put in the customer's name and address, along with contact name and job title if it's business-to-business. Always record the postcode and, where important, the telephone number. And please put it in accurately. People hate to see their names misspelt.

After that, the data you load will depend on the industry you are in, but for all industries key data is R, F, V, P:

- ❏ R – Recency. You need to know when a customer last ordered, so that you can send a rep back in or target a mailshot or special offer.
- ❏ F – Frequency. You need to know how frequently a customer orders, as that will identify your regular, loyal customers, who should be looked after very well.
- ❏ V – Value. You need to know how much a customer has spent cumulatively on a Moving Annual Turnover basis, and by individual order. Only you can decide whether a customer who regularly spends £500 a month is better to you than one who spends £5,000 twice a year.
- ❏ P – Product. You need to know what products a customer has bought in the last 12 months.

Case Study

Thomson Holidays

Product:

Preferred Agents.

Objectives:

Develop a direct communication cycle to drive customers to their Preferred Agent to book a Thomson holiday. To build brand awareness and maximize profits by promoting products and services.

Target market:

Thomson customers.

Offers:

Pre-departure customers – pre-book options and excursions, to save valuable holiday time.

Post-departure – Thomson Preferred Agents are the best place to buy a Thomson holiday; the customer gets an all-round better deal and can receive special Thomson offers.

Creative platform:

Due to the highly targeted nature of the campaign, the creative had to be clear and simple. It had to accommodate up to 184 different Preferred Agents' logos and 2,201 branch details as well as personalization by customer, resort and accommodation unit depending on the mailing channel. The creative needed to produce a template that would fit comfortably with the Thomson brand values, while simultaneously attracting interest.

Channels/Media:

The mail packs are produced using leading-edge digital printing – there are, in fact, 4,918,320 possible printing variants.

Results:

There are early indications of good response levels and customer reaction.

This is the start of your database. Other information you might load, depending on your business, would be the media source of that customer, the rep assigned, the sales territory in which he is located, what mailings he is receiving, how payment is made, whether there was a change of address recently, and any other data that helps you in marketing.

Remember, databases are for marketing. They are not the systems for the bean counters, the accountants. You build that database not for knowledge – although that is obviously attractive – but for future sales. Likewise, you do the same with prospects. Where did the lead come from? Who is the individual? What contact have they had with you since that initial enquiry? And then what?

Then you start to use it. Not all of your customers will buy all of your products all of the time, and mailing all of them, or calling on all of them regularly, is very expensive. Your database reduces your costs by enabling you to target your activity, for example:

❏ You are rationalizing your rep force, so you need to reduce the frequency of their calls. The database will tell you which customers are regular purchasers and should still be called on.

❏ You are launching a new product. It is similar to some of the products you already sell. You mail all the customers who have bought similar products in the last 12 months.

❏ You have a special monthly offer. You send it to everyone who has bought from the last three monthly offers. These people love a bargain and will buy, whatever it is.

❏ You are opening a new outlet. You invite everyone within 20 miles to a special opening event.

❑ You profile your existing customers and
   discover that their profile of characteristics is
   highly polarized. You apply that profile to the
   electoral roll and do a cold mailing to find new
   customers.

How do you update your database so that you don't run out of
computer space? Well, there are clever technical ways of making
more space, but the easiest is to take off those names and addresses
that are not working. Have a test programme on enquirers to see
how long it is worth holding their names and chasing them before
accepting that they are not interested. Then make that a definite cut-
off. Typically, this will be 18 months to four years, depending on the
product. Send them one last mailing before you chop them off.

With customers who stop purchasing, again keep chasing but
then send them a 'last-chance questionnaire', finding out why they
have stopped purchasing and getting them to ask to stay on the
mailing list.

The clever people then do clever modelling with statistical techniques such as CHAID, to predict who will respond, who will buy,
what they will buy. If you have a database of 500,000+ names, you
need the clever stuff. But if not, don't worry. Have a hugely
competent electronic filing cabinet – and make an effort to update it
regularly!

So, very simply, the concept of a database is your customers'
details stored in such a way that you can target offers to them, you
know their behaviour patterns as well as if they came into a shop
every week, and you can test and profitably exploit your dialogue
with them.

And guess what? Before you know it, you're running a 'loyalty
scheme', you're into 'relationship marketing', you're doing 'CRM'
(customer relationship management). These are all just fancy words
for milking your database.

13

A nice warm feeling, but . . .

You know what they say about corporate advertising. Like peeing down your trouser leg, it gives you a nice warm feeling but does nothing for anyone else. When we are talking about direct response advertising, we are talking about the exact opposite. Your warm feelings are irrelevant, and it's the performance of the ad that matters.

How do you increase the performance of your advertising? There are two main criteria: the media and the creative.

DIRECT-RESPONSE MEDIA

If you have a large enough budget, you should let an agency do the planning and buying for you. If not, read on! Planning and buying are equally critical. Planning, because you must know exactly why you are putting an ad where you are putting it, and buying, because the price you pay will have a direct effect on the end profitability of that ad.

In planning, the best tool you can have is your own historical data. If you haven't got any, start by defining your target audience, just as you would for direct mail. Do you want to reach consumers or businesses? Do you want to reach all consumers and all businesses, or do you want to segment by geography, lifestyle, social class and job title, industry type and company size?

Let's look at consumers first. Naturally, your most cost-effective route is national media, and particularly newspapers and magazines. (As a first-time user, you are unlikely to be looking at TV and radio.) Your media choice may be automatic – 'I want to sell a baby product, so I will go in mother and baby publications' – but it may be less obvious. For example, if you want to reach older, up-market couples, you will have to do more digging. Your starting point is BRAD (British Rate & Data). This is a monthly digest of every publication in the UK – thousands and thousands of titles, all segmented by category – that will tell you all the titles that are relevant for your market. You might want a list of something as obvious as all the Sunday quality news-papers or all the women's magazines, but you may be looking for more obscure titles. BRAD will give you some basic information on circulation and cost, but the thing to do is ring the publications up and ask for a media pack. These will give you extensive input on who takes the publication and what their profile is.

There are also two very helpful research surveys. National Readership Survey (NRS) surveys the profile of people who read the major papers and magazines in the UK. Target Group Index (TGI) researches adults on their purchasing patterns, and corre-lates who buys what with what they read. Both are cross-tabulated with the ACORN-type profiles (*see* pages 50–57), which can give you even more accurate pictures. You will probably need to use an agency to get hold of NRS and TGI data, as it comes on subscription.

Given all this data, you should then be able to draw up a 'candidate media schedule'. This will not necessarily be your final selection, but you will make your final selection from it. At this point, you need to consider the following:

❑ Cost – can you afford to advertise in the various titles?

❑ Circulation – is it large enough to give you the response you require, or is it so large that it might inundate you?

❑ Lead time (copy date) – you might need something to appear sooner rather than later or you might not have your ad ready for a couple of weeks, by which time you could have missed another issue, particularly on monthlies.

Case Study

Alliance & Leicester

Product:

Unsecured personal loans.

Background:

In a highly competitive market, market share has to come from 'cold' rather than 'warm' opportunities.

Objective:

To sell more loans via a consolidation message rather than the traditional route of cars or home improvements.

Challenge:

Difficult concept to explain.

Target market:

Creditworthy B, C1, C2 households.

Offer:

Debt consolidation loans at a very competitive rate.

Creative platform:

Strong imagery used to create impact and awareness.

Channels/Media:

Inserts placed in a mix of specialist and general titles, direct mail to in-house lists and lifestyle/mail order lists, and 48-sheet posters.

Results:

	Target loans issued index	Actual loans issued index
Inserts	100	263
Direct mail	100	232
Total	100	242

THE AD

Now, still at the planning stage, you need to decide what type of ad you are going to run. Your first decision is whether it is one-stage or two-stage. Are you looking for immediate commitment, cash with order, and so on, or are you looking for an enquiry? If it's one-stage, you may need to get clearance under the Mail Order Protection Scheme, which involves a lot of form-filling. (You will actually need MOPS clearance for all national newspapers and most of the major magazines.)

You will also need to decide whether you are going to use display (an ad in the run of the publication) or classified (a postal bargain ad in the classified section). Obviously, postal bargains are substantially cheaper and very good for testing, but you need to be selling a relatively cheap item, under £15–£20, to make it work.

If you are going to use two-stage, you will need to decide whether to use space or inserts. Space has more authority and more credibility, as your message sits alongside news and articles, but you pay the price for reaching all the readers. Inserts have the beauty of being able to be taken as part runs; for example, a magazine with a circulation of over one million may require you to supply only 50,000 inserts on a test run. This means that it's a lot cheaper and, for the same money, you can test many different titles.

Once you've chosen your titles, decided on your strategy and know your format, you need to consider size and position. Don't spend more than you have to in your early days. If you can communicate in a 15 x 2cm-column, don't buy a 25 x 4cm-column. Clearly, this depends on how well known you are and what your proposition is. In terms of position, do you need to be opposite the TV programme listings or the crossword for greater visibility? Do you want to reach men, and believe the sports page will be better for this? If you're taking a part insert run, do you want it randomly distributed or aimed at one geographical area?

The day of the week may matter to you as well if you are using national papers. Financial propositions work well at weekends, when there is more time to study the story, but a lot of direct marketing works best in the early part of the week, when there is less retail advertising 'cluttering the publication'.

If you are planning national business-to-business advertising, most of what I have said also applies. You won't get the same depth of research information in BRAD, but you will get a very wide choice of both vertical and horizontal media.

REGIONAL OPPORTUNITIES

On both consumer and business, if you don't want to go national your choice is more restricted. There are regional opportunities in many national publications, for example *Radio Times* and *TV Times*, but quite often only for inserts. There are also regional business magazines, but they don't tend to be very responsive. At a local level, newspapers are not good for direct response other than inserts in free sheets. Likewise, Chamber of Commerce publications are not very responsive. At a local level, it's often better to use direct mail.

Case Study

Royal Life

Product:

PEP.

Objective:

To generate leads.

Challenge:

Make PEPs interesting.

Target market:

B, C1 adults 45+.

Offer:

An award-winning PEP.

Creative platform:

Split run test of two approaches. The fund and its award, versus an unhappy consumer.

Channels/Media:

National press.

Results:

Man beat dog dramatically, ie benefit beat feature (see p 113).

DRTV

Finally, TV and radio are used more and more in conjunction with 'pure' direct marketing campaigns, either to pull a response in their own right or to influence more response from ads, mailings etc.

Some useful tips for DRTV are:

❑ Have a non-sexy, non-glamorous commercial – you're asking people to react to a simple, clear product message – and keep showing and repeating the phone number.

❑ Use low-coverage channels such as satellite and cable, so that the response can be handled either via live operators or voice-activated systems. Up to 25 per cent of DRTV responses are typically lost because callers cannot get through after a peak-time appearance.

❑ Turn your response round quickly – TV is a medium of immediacy.

14

How to get the best from your media buying

Media buying is the interface between the media plan and media owners. In order to execute the media plan so that the client gets maximum performance out of the advertising 'investment' (the budget), the buyer must use the 'Rate Card', the 'Mate Card' and the 'Late Card'.

THE RATE CARD

The Rate Card is the media owner's initial sales pitch. The media owner, whether selling lists, press, door-to-door distribution, broadcast or outdoor, will evaluate what the market coverage offered by the media product is worth. Cost ratios on audience coverage are affected by rival media opportunities. Usually, the more exclusive a market is, the higher the cost of entry. Rate Cards are structured so that the media owner will charge more for prime audience delivery, for example actives on a list, peak viewing segments on television Rate Cards, or special positions within the press.

Rate Cards stipulate a minimum price of entry and work up to offer incentives for volume spend. The buyer's first step is to understand the options and the flexibility available on the Rate Card. However, the Rate Card must never be taken as 'gospel', and planners and buyers alike must explore every opportunity to get the best value out of a media opportunity.

AN AGENCY'S MOST FLAMBOYANT AND FRIENDLY CREATURE –
THE MEDIA DIRECTOR

Case Study

Alliance & Leicester

Product:

Money Back Credit Card. The launch of a new credit card, unique in the UK, which offers money back on every purchase, every year.

Objective:

Generate one- and two-stage credit card applications via phone and post, as well as via A&L branches.

Target market:

Holders of other credit cards.

Creative platform:

The visual imagery used focused entirely on the card itself, and used the A&L orange and blue balls to maximum effect.

Channels/Media:

❑ consumer direct mail (cold);
❑ warm direct mail to A&L customers and staff;
❑ targeted door drops;
❑ teaser and direct response press ads;
❑ one- and two-stage media inserts;
❑ branch POS;
❑ radio;
❑ outdoor.

Results:

	Target index	Actual index
Enquiries	100	1,150
Cardholders	100	836
Balance transfers	100	583
Usage	100	212
Cost per card	100	73

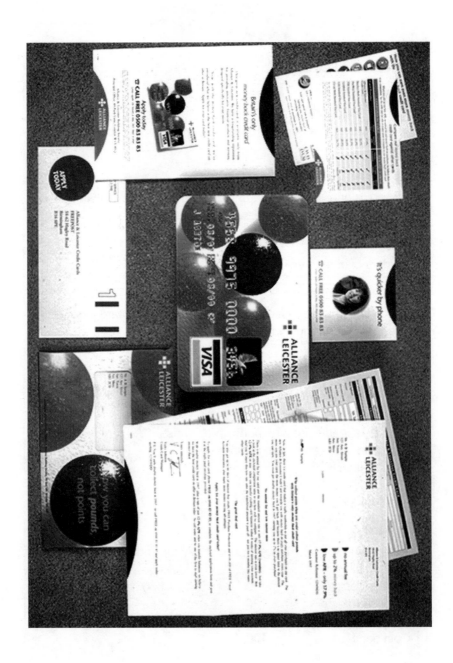

THE MATE CARD

At the next stage, the Mate Card is encountered. This is the relationship that media buyers (most likely your agency, rather than you) have with media owners. The relationship is vital to the effective execution of the media plan. The media owner and the media buyer rely upon each other. The media owner needs revenue, while the buyer needs the media commodity on the conditions and at the cost that will produce the best results for the advertiser. If this liaison isn't successful, the media representatives may be called into the sales director's office and will be asked, 'Why aren't we carrying this business?' There had better be a good reason! More often than not the answer will be down to cost, or an intricate buying strategy.

If an advertiser is to get maximum mileage out of media money, the buyer and the media owner must co-operate to the full. Media owner sales forces sell their product every day. They know it inside out. They are fully aware of which advertisers renew bookings and the reasons why advertisers pull out. Both media owners and buyers have a common objective – a successful campaign means more business.

Direct response media buying relies heavily on the Mate Card. During negotiations, the media buyer must tie down all the variables that will affect the response for each item of media that is bought on a schedule. The specifics are crucial and make the difference between a campaign that performs and one that bombs out!

Position is one of the essential variables that the direct response media buyer should consider. The buyer must position ads in the most suitable place in order to catch the target market. Direct response advertising results can be increased by 100 per cent if the ad is placed within relevant editorial. Often it can be worth investing in guaranteed positions if you can't negotiate them free of charge; cost premiums to guarantee positions usually range from 10–20 per cent, but your investment will pay off. The position on the page is also vital. Couponed ads must be placed so that prospects can clip them easily. The coupon must be on a cutting edge; if your coupon backs on to another couponed ad, you have been put into a situation of artificial competition and your results will suffer.

Sources of response are volatile, so you must continually test position as the opportunity arises. Many media owners can now provide 'Tip On' cards to be placed on an ad, instead of or as well as a coupon. These are so-called because they are inserts glued or 'tipped' on to an ad, and can take many different forms – from reply cards to mini catalogues. Tip Ons will involve an extra cost per thousand that will need to be evaluated within the buying equation. The Tip On facility can uplift conventional coupon results by more than 30 per cent, simply because they make the respondents' task easier, and they provide additional impact to the page.

Loose and bound-in inserts offer the media buyer an opportunity to conduct very cost-effective tests, either against space or in alternative media opportunities. Inserts also enable regionality, so the buyer can be very strategic and tailor the campaign to geographical areas containing prime markets. After testing, the buyer must analyse results and can then make a single cost-based decision on whether to roll out.

THE LATE CARD

The Late Card is the last ditch. Agencies have to be capable of taking last-minute deals from the media. The media owner benefits by gaining revenue. The agency can test opportunities at a low cost. The client obtains the benefits of a test and additional coverage/revenue at the lowest possible cost. All media plans that deserve the title 'plan' will cater for the eventuality of the Late Card, and will keep a contingency budget to make use of the opportunities that arise during the life of a campaign.

Case Study

Family Assurance Society

Product:

Family Bond.

Background:

The Family Assurance Society's Family Bond is a ten-year tax-free savings plan available to anyone between the ages of 18 and 70. Limited by the Government to one per adult, the maximum investment, at the time of this campaign (1991), was £13.50 per month, £150 per year, or a lump sum of £1,125.

Objective:

To generate both one- and two-stage response through broadcast and various support media.

Target market:

The Family Bond is affordable to most adults and has, therefore, a mass market appeal. However, there is a bias towards ABC1 adults with more 'up-market' lifestyles, aged 35–55.

Creative platform:

Creative across all the media used was consistent using the 'I've got one' theme.

Channels/Media:

Television, direct mail, door-to-door, inserts in the *TV Times*, 48-sheet posters, and national press advertisements.

Results:

The appearance of TV and posters at the same time as the other direct marketing activity created uplifts in the direct measurable response of the direct marketing activity: 200 per cent for inserts, 478 per cent for direct mail. TV and posters also produced enquiries in their own right, but the main objective of these media was to increase awareness.

PERFORMANCE AND RATES

The media planning and buying function should be integrated, when the plan is to maximize the potential to be derived from the budget. Media planners and buyers working on direct response-driven accounts operate with a major advantage over their brand advertising counterparts. This advantage is accountability.

The historical performance of direct marketing media activity provides the media planner and the media buyer with a hard base of fact. Statistics on media performance, in terms of ad size, position, timing, resultant enquiries/application and conversion rates, enable the media decision to be finite. The buyer can ultimately name the price at which it will be effective to buy. The break-even point can be established, and profitability is measurable.

TGI and NRS are widely used by media owners and agencies for justifying expenditure. Both sources of research are continually under the microscope of the major brand advertisers. Agencies are constantly criticizing the way in which research is conducted, and the media constantly complain about their positioning in the surveys.

In direct marketing, the picture is somewhat different. The direct response media buyer can use TGI, NRS and historic data in order to buy media at the right rates. Each client that a direct-marketing agency handles has a particular target market and a catalogue of response against front-end media costs. The only medium that delivers a 'pure' prime market for a direct-response advertiser is the database. Any further media usage involves considerable investment because, whatever media are selected, there will always be wastage. However, through sophisticated planning and strategic buying, customer recruitment through media activity can be cost-effective and is an essential means of growth for clients.

15

Generating response from advertising

The easiest way to generate response from advertising is to ask for it. That may sound trite, but it is absolutely true. Why should people respond to advertising if you don't ask them to? And the clearer your request, the more response you will get. Other subtleties come into play, and we will consider them all, but first let's refresh ourselves on the type of advertising available for most small firms and DIYers: space and inserts.

With space advertising, you can buy either classified or display. Classified is obviously the cheapest, but your response opportunities are reduced as, at best, you can show a response address and telephone number, but no coupon or additional sales message. For a low-grade, cheap-price proposition it could work. Do your competitors use it?

More commonly, display advertising is used, with an ad sitting among editorial. In this case, you have to decide very early whether you are going to use one-stage or two-stage. That is, are you asking the reader to place an order or to express interest in more information? If it's one-stage, you'll need a much larger ad – usually a full page. So what are the rules in one-stage, or 'off the page' as it is often called?

1. No clever headlines – tell it as it is, and give a description of the product and the price (very important).
2. Have a factual representation of the product. No line drawings. Always photographs. No 'mood' shots, where you can't see the product details.
3. If the product is complex, have some inset shots showing the detail.
4. Use extensive copy to describe the product offer in full. Here you must sell the steak as well as the sizzle.
5. Give clear ordering instructions. How do they fill in the order form? Can they order by telephone with a credit card or an account number?
6. A logical layout draws the eye from the product to the headline to the copy to the coupon.
7. Show credit card symbols – it uplifts response.

Case Study

Employment Department

Campaign:

National Training Awards.

Objectives:

To generate enquiries and entries for awards.

Challenges:

1. To explain a complex application process in a concise, powerful manner.
2. To cut through the clutter and attract sufficient interest and numbers for the awards from smaller firms.

Target market:

Personnel professionals and training managers in small to medium businesses.

Benefit:

To explain the prestige and status benefits gained by the winners, who are entitled to use the Government NTA symbol on their literature.

Creative platform:

Used a highly appropriate 'harvesting' theme throughout both visuals and copy. With a restricted budget dictating a three-colour approach, we used a warm illustration style to complement the theme, and clearly demonstrated to the target market exactly how they could 'reap the benefits' from winning these awards.

Channels/Media:

Direct-response inserts in a range of vertical industry media to reach smaller businesses.

Results:

Enquiries 120 per cent above target; entries 90 per cent above target.

The same rules apply in two-stage advertising, where you will probably have less space, as quarter- and half-pages usually do the job. In this case, you are selling the sizzle, not the steak, so you need an emotive (but not clever) headline:

- ❏ 'Why You Should Choose';
- ❏ 'How You Can Benefit From...';
- ❏ 'Free Offer to Readers of This Magazine'.

Follow the headline with summary copy that describes the proposition – 'Our new catalogue is now out'; 'This new product is now available' – and ask people to ask for more information. Don't imply it, say it! Show the product. If it's a catalogue, show the catalogue; if it's a service, show users benefiting from it. Then put a coupon in. Even if 90 per cent of your response is going to come over the phone, put a coupon in. Pattern recognition means the readers will realize that you are looking for response. Put obvious dotted lines around the coupon and make it rectangular, not a funny shape. Put strong copy in the coupon – 'Yes! Please send me. . .' – and, if you are encouraging telephone response, show a telephone symbol and a large clear number. Complete the coupon yourself, to make sure there is enough room to do so.

Inserts can be loose, bound-in or tipped on. Loose are the most common, as most magazines and newspapers will carry them. They often increase response because you have more space to tell the story, and because the recipient can post them straight back without having to find an envelope. You need to make an early decision about whether to use paper or card. In my view, if there is a lot of copy and maybe even an application form, paper is best, but ideally paper that folds up to make a self-contained reply paid card for a quick, instant response in large quantities.

If you are using paper, it is likely to be A4 folded to A5, as many publications will not take A4 size unfolded. If card, the three most popular formats are A6, A5 and L shape. A6 is just like a holiday postcard, and should be treated as such. Picture of proposition and headline on side one, and on side two the left-hand half carrying the message and the space for name and address, and the right-hand side the reply address. With A5, it is usual to have a portion at the bottom perforated to detach and return, so you have the opportunity to carry what are effectively two advertisements, one on either side. With an L shape, the only difference is that the reply portion sticks out and is more dominant.

Case Study

Nescafé

Product:

Launch of Espresso, an instant espresso in sachets.

Objectives:

To increase awareness of the product, generate product trial and gain market share.

Challenge:

The product was brand-new and unproven, with no data on the target market. We needed to combine response and brand building in the advertisement.

Target market:

B, C1 adults, aged 25–40 years, who are coffee drinkers and who may have espresso on holiday or in restaurants but do not drink it at home.

Offer:

A free trial pack.

Creative platform:

The ad was sophisticated and stylish with elements of intrigue and stimulation to reflect the product, together with heavy branding. Two-thirds of the ad was devoted to the brand and one-third to the response, which had an opt-in mechanism to get people to ask for a sample.

Channels/Media:

National press including *Radio Times*, *You* magazine, Sainsbury's magazine and *GQ*. Total circulation: 7,000,000.

Results:

Response was equivalent to 1 per cent of the circulation of each magazine used.

Bound-ins are literally bound into the magazine. They give you the opportunity for a mini-brochure equivalent, but not all publications take them and they can reduce response because they look like editorial. Tip Ons have a reply card 'tipped on' to a full-page advertisement. They are frightfully expensive, but some clients claim a tenfold response uplift.

Don't forget that the key to successful response advertising is to put the ad or the insert in the right publication in the first place. If you chase the wrong audience, the brilliance of your message and creative treatment will be irrelevant.

This is equally true with broadcast media. DRTV in particular needs clear, simple messages and *heavy* exposure of the phone number. On radio, keep repeating the phone number. On cinema, link to a take-one in the foyer. Likewise, if you are using the Web as an advertising channel, keep signalling the call to action – click here, phone me – whatever it is, keep ramming it down their throats.

16

Hey, you – I don't know your name

If you don't have access to the right lists, don't worry! Door-to-door and product despatch are great alternatives.

DOOR-TO-DOOR

Door-to-door is a highly flexible medium; the key benefit is that it is cheap. You might use companies who distribute freesheet newspapers or money-off vouchers. This is very cheap, but there is virtually no ability to target if you buy into a national 'shareplan' distribution. If your quantities are smaller, and you're prepared to pay a bit more, many companies will provide you with geodemographic (census-based profiling) selectability. However, your material still lands with others at some time during the day.

A key alternative is the Royal Mail door-to-door service, which delivers your material at the same time as the morning post. Targeting can be quite precise, as 'postal sector rankings' can be produced by the use of geodemographics. These enable you to target postal sectors with a high penetration of your perceived target audience, and to deliver to these sectors only. One postal sector includes approximately 1,000 households.

Creativity for door-to-door revolves around the fact that you

Case Study

Ronseal

Product:

Thompsons Water Seal.

Background:

Thompsons Water Seal protects bricks against water damage.

Objectives:

To educate consumers on the product and to encourage a visit to DIY retail outlets.

Challenge:

To track the effectiveness of direct marketing when retailers will not co-operate in redemption tracking.

Target market:

C1, C2, D males.

Offer:

Free prize draw in return for purchasing/awareness information.

Creative platform:

Factual, rational, male.

Channels/Media:

Door-to-door via newshare distribution targeted to a geodemographic profile.

Results:

Target response index: 100
Actual response index: 220
89 per cent of respondents said they would buy the product as a result of learning more about it.

cannot address individuals by name, so you must be tactical in an alternative way. Your creative direction is likely to be dictated by your distribution method. If you are doing a cheap mass-market exercise, you need to control your production costs. In such a case, a run-on of any existing media insert you already have is likely to prove cost-effective – remember the size of the average letterbox, though. It might be better to use an A6 or an L shape rather than something that gets folded and spoilt. Obviously, if you are in the 50p money-off game you should know what works anyway (if any of it *is* still working, with the current degree of saturation).

More importantly, there are genuine creative opportunities if you use Royal Mail door-to-door, because your material lands with the post. This is where I believe direct mail lookalike packs have a significant role to play. Start with a DL or C5 envelope, as anything larger may not be accepted. Overprint the envelope, not only with a sales message but also with a fake frank design to increase authenticity. Use a window envelope, as this increases the implication that it has been mailed and addressed.

Inside, enclose what you would normally put in a mail pack – at the very least, a letter, leaflet and response mechanism. The letter needs a non-personalized salutation, showing through the window. Try 'Hello there' or 'To the lady of the house'. Have some sort of mini-leaflet which shows your proposition; this can be two- or four-colour, depending on the product. In most cases, you should have a two-stage reply card (although I have made one-stage mini catalogues work). Watch your weight, and don't pay over the lowest threshold if you can help it.

For full creative input, the same rules apply as for direct mail and inserts.

Case Study

NatWest Insurance Services

Product:

Home and contents insurance.

Objectives:

To generate enquiries for quotes.

Challenges:

To position NWIS as different when really it was like all other insurance brokers.

Target market:

Existing NatWest customers.

Offer:

Try us out.

Creative platform:

Tested cuddly animals versus the strength of soldier and policeman.

Channels/Media:

Statement insert.

Results:

Soldier and policeman beat puppy and kitten. Serious beats cute when money is involved.

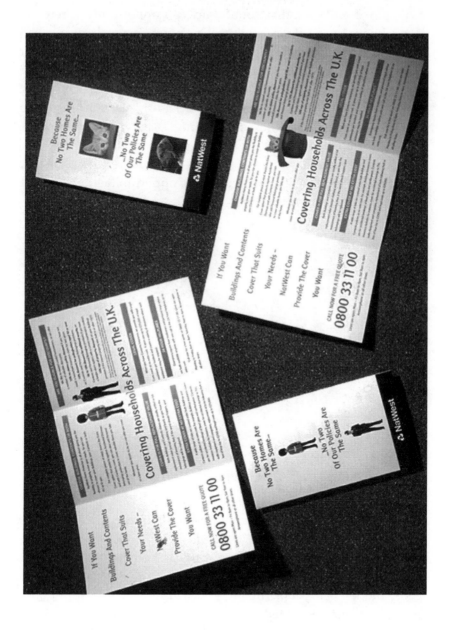

PRODUCT DESPATCH

Let's move on to another communication opportunity where we don't know the recipient's name – product despatch, also called 'third party' and 'piggybacks'. Very simply, this means putting your message out with other people's communication opportunities. For example, it might be sent with a parcel from a mail order company; with a statement mailing from a financial organization, such as a retail credit card provider or building society; with 'backend' product, such as a binder for a partwork series; or with one-offs, such as confirmation of theatre tickets booked over the phone by credit card. There are literally millions of opportunities here, if your profile matches that of the third party.

'WHEN I SAID "LET'S GET INTO BED WITH EACH OTHER..."'

Unsurprisingly, the majority of opportunities are in mail order. You won't get a perfect match, though. If you want to promote a gardening catalogue, it is unlikely that mail order gardening catalogues will take you. However, if you know that your gardeners also cook, the kitchen people might. You will find that most opportunities are female-related and, in the UK, often Midlands- or North-based, but not always. Consider military book clubs, binder buyers of partworks on car maintenance, London theatregoers, and you are quite likely to find what you want.

Do bear the following points in mind:

1. The third party does not want a massive uplift in postage, so will probably only accept a card as opposed to some sort of pack. If you plan on A6 you won't go far wrong.
2. They will not be able to guarantee you an exact despatch date; most programmes run in four-weekly cycles.
3. You won't be able to target more tightly than the programme in total; there is no ACORN-type selection here.

As long as you remember these limitations, if you are keen to try, there is no reason why you should not identify a number of companies and give them a go. They'll either say 'No, never', or 'We haven't done it before, but why not?', or 'Yes, but you must go through our broker', in which case they will tell you who is brokering their programmes. If you're not sure what you want, go direct to the brokers and ask them what they have available.

Remember, door-to-door and piggybacks offer many extra opportunities to be tactical with your direct marketing programmes. Don't turn your nose up at them. They give volume opportunities if you've saturated all other media. They give cheaper opportunities if you have a limited budget. They give local opportunities where lists aren't very good. And they can be very, very successful.

17

Bums on seats or bums off seats?

Most of the time we want our targets to be sat down reading our message. But sometimes we want them to stand up! Direct marketing can be used to get people to go somewhere, as well as to do something. However, because it usually requires more effort for us all to move ourselves from A to B, it follows that the motivator needs to be greater. This can range from a straight bribe, through a 'chance to win', and on to flattery and exclusivity.

EXCLUSIVITY

Everyone likes to feel special, and acknowledged, so the special invitation to the President's box, the VIP lounge, the gourmet supper, will always pull a higher response from your target prospects, whether they are consumers or businesses. However, don't forget the following:

1. Make sure it is genuinely exclusive and not for the 'herd', as you will quickly be found out.
2. Sustain the exclusivity with a quality mailing; this is one of the times when what I call the 'wedding invitation' pack works well.
3. Always ask for an RSVP.

Case Study

Drive Computing

Product:

Computer hardware and software resellers.

Objective:

To launch brand-new local business.

Challenge:

Crowded market; what's one more player?

Target market:

Local businesses within 50-mile (80-km) radius.

Offer:

Free seminar and free credit card guide.

Creative platform:

Tried to demystify the world of computers.

Channels/Media:

Cold direct mail.

Results:

Beat target on number of visitors.

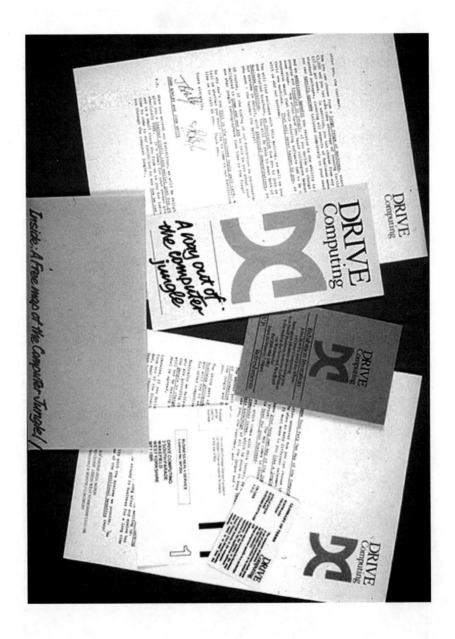

You can create an event – you don't need to wait until one actually exists. Make your own seminar, your own conference, your own restaurant sampling, your own shop's birthday party. Equally, you can piggyback on established activity. For example, if you can't afford a stand/booth at your industry's trade show, book a hotel room close by and invite your key prospects over for a drink. They will thank you for a chance to sit down!

'CHANCE TO WIN'

In my experience, using the 'chance to win' approach in order to move people physically towards you works less effectively than a guaranteed reward. We all love sweepstakes and free prize draws when we don't have to do anything but respond from our armchair/desk. However, it is much harder to motivate people to travel in return for a chance to win. By all means use the approach to gather names and addresses (for example, at a trade show) but don't rely on it to pull people.

Case Study

Bradford & Bingley Building Society

Product:

First time mortgages.

Objective:

To generate leads from first-time buyers.

Challenge:

To find 18- to 24-year-olds, particularly couples, who do not react to traditional media.

Target market:

Adults, aged 18 to 24 years, in the market for a mortgage.

Offer:

The Society is a good mortgagee and there was a free Argos voucher for every enquirer.

Creative platform:

Illustrative commercial on the anatomy of the first-time buyer – gently humorous.

Channels/Media:

Cinema. The UK's first-ever direct response cinema commercial. Message routed prospects to cinema foyer on their way out to collect a leaflet which doubled up as redemption voucher on incentive, when they visited a Bradford & Bingley branch.

Results:

The cost per new mortgage was cheaper than traditional channels.

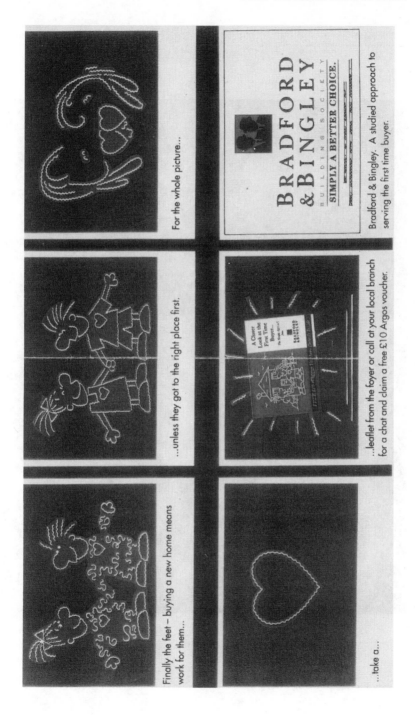

BRIBES

If you can't or don't want to use the VIP route, don't be too proud – go for the bribe. It doesn't have to be expensive. Think 'cute', 'unusual', 'gimmick'. What about weird clocks, personal organizers, pocket radios, adult toys, printed guides to currencies or wine or airlines, cartoons or pictures? Just think what you yourself would quite fancy.

Don't use refreshment as the 'freebie'. Common courtesy says you should give a cup of tea or a glass of wine, and a biscuit or sandwich if people have made the effort to come to you.

Don't forget this area of direct marketing – marketing which *directs* your prospects to you.

18

Does your campaign have the ring of success?

Telemarketing by direct marketers is becoming increasingly common, but what is it, and what could it do for you?

Telemarketing is using the telephone to provide a direct link between company and customer or prospect, rather than using the conventional mail or sales representative mechanisms. Telemarketing can refer to incoming or outgoing communication by the telephone. The great advantages of the telephone are that it is flexible and live, and that it allows two-way communication. It gives the ultimate direct link between company and consumer, and is undoubtedly the direct marketing technique with quickest available response rate.

What are the advantages offered by the speed of telemarketing? It allows a salesperson to make many, many more calls in a day. This means that it is considerably cheaper to operate, so it's cost efficient for the salesperson to operate even on the most marginal accounts. It allows any salesperson to reach any town in the country on the same day. The telephone has no geographic restrictions, and allows anyone to be represented in London, Leeds, Luton or Liverpool, all within an hour. It allows a salesperson to increase the value of an order by cross-selling/upselling, and to convert an enquiry to an order on the spot.

Many of our clients ask me what telemarketing can be used for. The answer is simple: anything. I regularly recommend it for:

❑ following up mail shots of expensive products;
❑ taking orders;
❑ validating lists;
❑ keeping in touch with marginal accounts;
❑ arranging meetings and appointments;
❑ customer communication – tell them there's a sale on now!

'DO YOU HAVE TROUBLE SLEEPING, SIR? MAY I TAKE THIS OPPORTUNITY TO INTRODUCE YOU TO SLUMBEEZY MATTRESSES?'

Case Study

Lakeland Limited

Product:

Kitchen products.

Background:

Lakeland Limited is a mail order company selling kitchen-related products via catalogue. Lakeland Limited was the first kitchen catalogue advertiser to test DRTV in the UK.

Objectives:

To test DRTV as a recruitment channel, and establish the viability of television advertising in this marketplace. To generate quality catalogue requests from a discerning female audience, at a cost-effective rate.

Target market:

Airtime delivery was geared towards an up-market housewife audience.

Offer:

Send for a catalogue.

Creative platform:

The catalogue was used as the 'hero' of the ad, using a striking visual technique. The catalogue 'morphed' into a front door, which opened to allow the customer into the world of Lakeland products, which seamlessly transformed into one another before trans-forming back to the catalogue cover.

Channels/Media:

Television – Channel 4, South Macro; ITV, Grampian; Satellite, Sky 1, Sky News, Discovery, Home & Leisure, and UK Living.

Results:

Total order value: 20 per cent above target.

Take care, however. I would never recommend using a telemarketing campaign to cold consumers (although it works well in a business-to-business context). It can cause irritation, create ill will and disrupt people's privacy. Indeed, it is now unlawful in many circumstances.

Arguably, telemarketing is more suitable for selling services than tangible products; it is hard to sell an object that cannot be seen. For this reason, I recommend using telemarketing as a back-up medium, for following up mailshots on which the product has been pictured, or for taking orders from customers. Telemarketing is at its best when a number is given in press, TV or Internet advertising as a source for further information. From this position, the skilled tele-operator is dealing straight away with a consumer in a 'thinking of buying' frame of mind. I would always recommend using telemarketing in the warmest possible environment.

A good example of how consumers have warmed to the telephone is provided by the mail order companies. All of them now take more orders by telephone than by post.

A TELEMARKETING CAMPAIGN

How do you set up a telemarketing campaign? That is, an outbound campaign to generate business, rather than an inbound one to process business. The major point to remember is to treat this medium just like any other direct marketing technique.

Don't forget the rules of direct mail and databases – personalization and customer knowledge really count. They are always important, but never more so than when your operatives are in a two-way dialogue. It is also important to know your own company, which is why updated stock levels are such an asset for telesales staff taking orders for mail order companies.

What makes a good telemarketing campaign? The major point to remember is that the operator represents your company, and first impressions count. If you use a telemarketing company, they will know this. However, if you plan to use Gloria on the switchboard when she's got a spare half hour, be very careful. I always recommend a script, which involves an opening statement or opening evidence of your company, followed by questions that are structured to require more than a one-word 'Yes' or 'No' answer. Communication is self-evidently vital on the telephone – it's a two-way medium – and open-ended questions open a conversation.

From there on, it is best to give your operators pointers to talk about, rather than a definite speech. Pointers or prompts allow a conversation to build naturally, giving skilled tele-operators the opportunity to use their initiative, rather than forcing them into problems when a conversation doesn't fall into a specific pre-arranged pattern. It is imperative that the operator speaks clearly and with precise diction – mumbling is unacceptable – and does not smoke or eat while on the phone. Your image is at stake. It doesn't matter whether your telesales people wear three-piece suits or their birthday suits, but their voices can pass on enthusiasm and professionalism, or apathy and insincerity.

It is just as important to be able to listen as to talk, and a professional telephone operator should be able to handle any situation, even when the party at the other end is complaining, or even bordering on the abusive. A good telemarketing agency should train its staff to handle every situation with tact and efficiency, taking down any complaint carefully for the correct follow-up procedures to take place.

Timing is important, too. If you are operating a consumer programme, it is pointless ringing in the morning. Look to phone between 7 and 9pm, when your consumer will be at home and not at work. Check that this is allowed under the new legislation and, in any case, don't phone cold. If you are operating a business-to-business campaign, or if you are looking to make appointments by phone, ring within business hours. When running an order-taking system for consumers, don't be frightened to run your system in the evenings or at weekends when your customers are in. Look at the big mail order houses – they are open for orders at 4am!

Further proof of the power of the telephone is given by the success of 0800 and other 'free' numbers. Just look at the Sunday supplements and count how many times an 0800 number is used as the response mechanism. Dial-for-details is a proven winner in the industry. Dial-for-details-free generally gives that extra lift to response. I'm sure you will find the cost of the calls is worth it for the extra response – but make sure you can handle the response.

Direct marketing by the telephone sounds like an easy concept but, like all other techniques available within the industry, it needs careful planning and execution. Remember the value of personalization, personality, enthusiasm, timing and customer knowledge and you have all the basics to ring in success!

19

Web-wise or Web-weary?

The Internet can be used either for awareness or for transactions (or both). Unless you are already operating as a mail order/catalogue company, you should think very seriously before trading on the Internet. You must have your systems – stock, warehousing, order fulfilment, payment, returns, refunds – in place and tested first. If you were to cut your teeth on all that and the Net at the same time, you'd die! (OK, I know Amazon did it, but they haven't made much money and they have spent a fortune.)

If you are a mail order operator, you should get into e-commerce, but don't let common sense fly out of the window just because it's the brave new world of technology. The same old rule applies – KISS! What are you selling, how much is it, and how do I order it? Will my credit card be secure? Will you acknowledge my order so I know it's not floating around in the ether somewhere? When will my goods arrive? If I'm in a different country, what happens if the goods are faulty, or I don't like them? Never *launch* a mail order business on the Internet – only *transfer* one!

If you're a regular two-stage advertiser, you want leads and enquiries and prospects and quotes, so the Internet should be added to your list of media of first choice. However, do make it not only pleasant, but easy too. Of course your online ad can have all sorts of sexy graphics and animation, but if it takes five minutes to download, I'm going to get bored.

Remember, a lot of advertising works because people like browsing. We flip passively through tons of received messages until one actively catches our eye. Your online ad needs to work in the same way. If it's slow to build and complex to follow – and unclear in its primary messages – not only will you get no response, but you may also create a negative reaction.

Use the Internet judiciously, and don't be intimidated by its technology. And remember, most UK households are still not 'wired' and even those that are use it randomly. It will be a long time before it becomes the prime response tool for mass-market (as opposed to early-adopter) consumers. In business-to-business, on the other hand, it's a given that a company needs its own Web site, which must at the very least function as a corporate ad and brochure.

Indeed, it makes a great deal of sense to use direct marketing to drive prospects to your Web site rather than investing marketing money in glossy brochures. Exploit the Internet's penetration to give you as much of a profile as your larger competitors, but don't trade online unless you are very confident.

Case Study

Department of Trade and Industry

Product:

Web site for exporters.

Objectives:

1. To raise awareness of the DTI's exporters' Web site.
2. To explain the benefits.
3. To increase usage from new and experienced exporters, especially SMEs.

Challenge:

To provide an innovative solution using traditional channels to promote a Web site cost effectively.

Target market:

Current and potential exporting companies.

Offer:

To visit the DTI's Web site, and to complete a short questionnaire for the chance to win £1,000 worth of export support.

Creative platform:

Bright and colourful to attract attention.

Channels/Media:

Several channels were used to reach the target audience:

1. Mail;
2. Loose inserts;
3. Card decks;
4. Classified advertising;
5. Web site banner.

Results:

During the four months following the campaign the Web site hits per month were 66 per cent above pre-campaign levels.

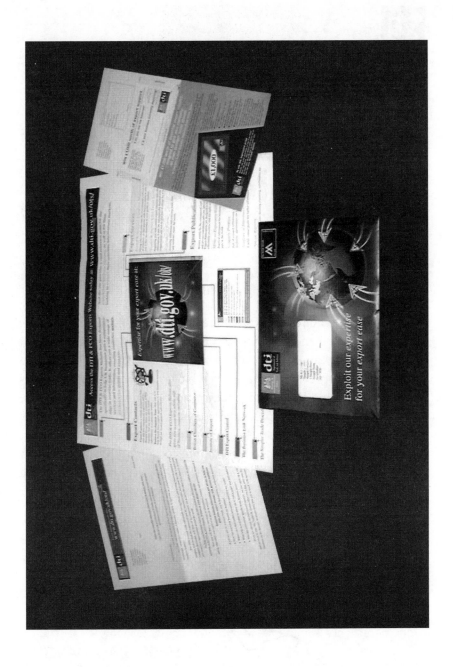

20

A catalogue of errors or a catalogue of success?

For many direct marketers, catalogues are the life blood of revenue. They are the shop and the shop window, the alternative retail outlets, but many companies, particularly those new to the game, fail to maximize the opportunity created by what is not a cheap exercise. This is most noticeable in a retail environment, where catalogues are conceptually seen as sales promotion devices. All well and good if they are only intended to support the drive into the retail outlet (although I would still question the investment), but too many retailers try and piggyback a mail order service on these catalogues without applying the rules which make mail order catalogues work best.

ALL-SINGING, ALL-DANCING
CATALOGUE

Case Study

BT

Product:

Catalogue.

Background:

BT is one of the leading providers of business telecommunications equipment and services. The catalogue showed a range of BT's products and services.

Objectives:

1. To support channel management of the Small Business Segment (SBS) which maximizes revenue opportunities while containing costs.
2. To reinforce the BT brand in this vital business sector.
3. To sell products and services.

Challenge:

The challenge was to change the approach to make it a genuine 'mail order' operation, with catalogue rules and disciplines.

Target market:

Small- and medium-sized enterprises (SMEs).

Creative platform:

An abstract image was incorporated on all pieces in the mailing. This would be unexpected and dramatic, but still relevant, as BT's hardware would be ghosted on to the visual.

Channels/Media:

The in-house database was mailed.

Results:

Response was 25 per cent ahead of target.

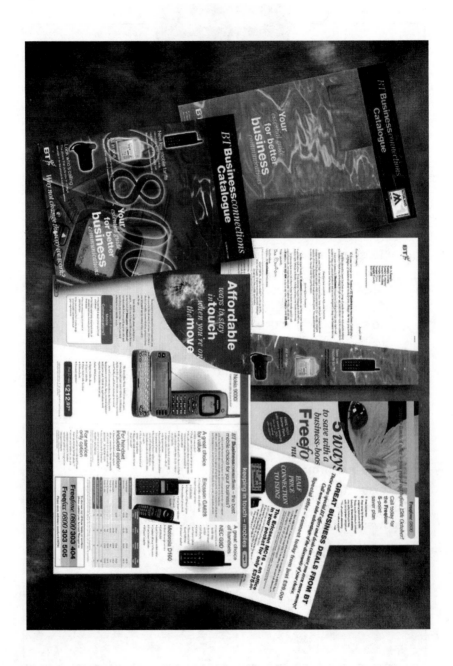

Obviously, all rules are flexible and will be adapted, depending on whether you are talking about an eight-page A5 or an 800-page A4. However, in my experience, the fundamental shapes and disciplines need to be there, whatever the size, and whatever the market, because you are selling, not talking. For example, for one client I achieved an uplift of sales of over 90 per cent by applying consumer catalogue techniques to a business catalogue.

What are these all-important rules? Leaving aside merchandise selection, which should be the prerogative of the brand and product managers and the buyers, let's talk about the production of the catalogue.

Surprisingly, the starting point is not the design but the pagination – what has to go where. A re-paginated catalogue with no change to product or design can uplift sales by as much as 30 per cent. Pagination means determining:

- ❏ how many pages to a product section;
- ❏ how many products to a page within a section;
- ❏ what order the sections appear in;
- ❏ what order on the page the product appears in.

How is this done? Well, ideally, it should be based on previous years' or seasons' experiences. Hard data works here, not opinion. Every catalogue has 'hot spots', which are pages where sales will be greater because of the way a reader reads a catalogue. The hot spots are, in order of importance:

1. front cover;
2. back cover;
3. inside front cover;
4. inside back cover;
5. pages 2, 3 and 4;
6. centre spread (so long as the pages are sewn or stapled to the cover).

Case Study

Heather Valley

Product:

Home shopping catalogue.

Objective:

To increase sales.

Challenge:

To increase catalogue sales without increasing production costs.

Target market:

Older ladies.

Offer:

Nice fashion.

Creative platform:

Catalogue was taken from 64 pages of A5 to 32 pages of A4.

Channels/Media:

House file direct mail.

Results:

Increase in sales by 17 per cent.

The hot spots should be allocated to your high-selling merchandise, your best-sellers or your very expensive items. The balance of the book should then be paginated in descending order by value forecast. The number of pages allocated to a section will be determined by the number of products you have to sell in that section, as there will be a level of page density beyond which you cannot go. But remember – paginate the sections first and then the individual pages within the section.

When it comes to the position of a product on a page, two factors come into play. The value of the product, which will dictate the amount of space you allocate to it, and the known eye movement patterns, which will dictate where on the page the product sits.

Remember that catalogues function as spreads, not pages, so left- and right-hand pages should be planned jointly. Eye movement research shows that the eye starts top right of the right-hand page, moves across to the join between the two pages (the 'gutter') and out again to the bottom right of the right-hand page. The eye will only look at the left-hand page if it is visually led to do so. This is done either by carrying across the overall design theme, or by having a stackable product – a row of plates, for example – actually straddling the gutter, to lead the eye across.

In addition to hot spots, catalogues also benefit from stop pages. These are special pages – maximum every eight, minimum every 20 – where the reader is 'stopped' by a special offer, or an introduction to a new section, or a change in design. This is one occasion where you plan by page, not by spread, always using a right-hand page.

Catalogue photography is absolutely key as well. The products must be the heroes. You may like that moody night shot of a woman's suit, but if the customer can't see that it's a suit and not a dress because it's dark around the waistline, or that it has three pockets and specially shaped sleeves, then sales will go down or returns will go up. The costs of handling returns have broken many a catalogue virgin. Without being uncreative, catalogue photography must show the product very clearly, and if it is complex or has many features, small inset shots will often help.

Catalogue copy is crucial too. Here, you must remember that you need selling copy as well as product copy. Obviously, you must describe the product accurately, but if you use creative copy which sells the sizzle as well as the sausage, people will be more inclined to purchase. To this extent, headlines and flashes – 'New', 'Special Offer', 'Two for the price of one' – are intrinsic to the copy proposition.

When it comes to putting it all together on the page, don't have your text too far from your picture. People should not have to search to find the words that go with the picture. Code each product shot clearly, and if you are using an Alpha sequence it is often better to start again on the right-hand page of a spread. People have better pattern recognition of A B C D E than they do of M N O P Q. Don't put the price alongside or on top of the photograph unless it is a special offer, but do show the price clearly in bold type alongside the product code.

Other points? It is useful to have a policy page (usually page 2) where you introduce people to the catalogue, talk about anything particularly exciting, show an index or contents, and show your guarantee (very important). You should also have a 'How to order' section, which can go at the front or the back. You may think it's obvious, but you would be surprised how many people are unsure how to complete order forms or order by telephone unless it is explained.

Many catalogues bind an order form into the centre of the catalogue. This has the advantage of providing more than one order form, an opportunity for extra sales of 'little' items, from one-colour line drawings, and even a solicitation to recommend a friend. The disadvantage is that you cannot code by customer or group for accurate tracing without putting up your production costs substantially, so you will have to rely on your database. Also, you lose the centre spread as a hot spot. If that happens, you need to treat the pages before and after the order forms as one-offs, where it is often worth including low-value items for impulse sales.

This is a brief summary of some key catalogue points. If you are new to catalogues you could do a lot worse than look at those from the big mail order houses – they know the rules. If you are going to invest thousands in a catalogue, make sure it sells, and doesn't just look pretty.

21

Measuring direct marketing

Direct marketing is about measurement. What does that mean? Well, obviously it depends on your objectives, but a simple model might be:

Campaign cost	£10,000
Enquiries	1,000
Cost per enquiry (CPE)	£10
Customers	500
Conversion rate	50%
Cost per customer (CPC)	£20

On its own, that means nothing, but as a benchmark it's priceless, because it's about comparators, not absolutes. Is £10 CPE from direct mail better or worse than from ads or inserts? Is £10 from an accountant's list better or worse than the equivalent from an IT director's list? Does the *Daily Mail* or the *Daily Express* pull better?

Remember, leads are a means to an end, not an end in their own right. Was the price you paid for a customer profitable from the margin on the first order, or do you need two or three or four orders before you get into profit after the DM costs?

Let's look at two hypothetical models.

EXAMPLE ONE

Proposition: Ring and ask for a quote for car insurance.

Mailing volume:	100,000
Mailing cost:	£50,000
Mailing response:	0.3%
Enquiry for quote:	300
Cost per enquiry:	£167
Rejected by company:	0%
Rejected by punter:	40%
Converted to customer:	50%
Number of customers:	150
Cost per customer:	£333

If a typical car insurance policy is for £300, and the margin to the client is 40 per cent, ie £120, then the client needs to keep the customer for three years to break even, and into a fourth year to make a profit.

There are four ways this depressing situation can be improved. Work these out for yourself and see which is the best way forward.

i Mail a better list. Increase initial response to 0.5% and conversion to 60%.

ii Mail a better list with a better pack. Increase initial response to 0.75% (and conversion to 60%) but increase mailing costs to £70,000.

iii Mail a cheaper pack. Reduce mailing costs to £35,000.

iv Drop prices and slacken criteria. Increase conversion rate to 75%. Client rejects down to 3%, customer rejects down to 22%.

	i	ii	iii	iv
Mailing volume	100,000	100,000	100,000	100,000
Mailing cost	£50,000	£70,000	£35,000	£50,000
Mailing response	0.5%	0.75%	0.3%	0.3%
Enquiry for quote	£500	£750	£300	£300
Cost per enquiry	£100	£93	£117	£117
Rejected by client	10%	10%	10%	3%
Rejected by customer	30%	30%	40%	22%
Converted	60%	60%	50%	75%
Number of customers	300	450	150	255
Cost per customer	£167	£156	£233	£222
Break even	Year 2	Year 2	Year 2	Year 2
Profit	Year 3	Year 3	Year 3	Year 3

EXAMPLE TWO

Proposition: Order this set of pans for £39.99 from this insert in this magazine.

Insert volume:	500,000
Insert cost (media):	£11,000
Insert cost (print):	£15,000
Insert cost (total):	£26,000
Response:	0.1%
Orders:	500
Cost per order:	£52

The margin on the pans is 70 per cent. There is also some margin in the postage and packing charges. The client earns £29 from every set sold. Thus, for every £1 spent on marketing the client recovers only 56 pence. The ideal is to get £1 back for £1 spent (break even), as the customer can be made profitable on future sales.

Which of these examples achieves break even?

> i Increase insert volume to two million by reducing print unit costs to £20 per 1,000.
> ii Reduce print costs to £15 per 1,000 by reducing size and quality of insert. Will reduce response rate to 0.075%.
> iii Change magazines to increase response rate to 0.2%.

	i	ii	iii
Insert volume	2,000,000	500,000	500,000
Insert cost (media)	£44,000	£11,000	£11,000
Insert cost (print)	£40,000	£7,500	£15,000
Insert cost (total)	£84,000	£18,500	£26,000
Response	0.1%	0.075%	0.2%
Orders	2,000	375	1,000
Cost per order	£42	£49	£26
Return on investment (ROI) per £	69p	70p	£1.11

The one thing you never, never, never measure is pure percentage response. Without the money, it's meaningless. I can get 100 per cent response if I offer every respondent a £5 note. I can be profitable on 0.05 per cent response if the margin is there.

Remember, too, that direct marketing is not a one-hit wonder. What we want is regular customers – in other words, lifetime value. If I shop at the supermarket every week and spend £100 and I do that for 20 years, my lifetime value is £104,000. Isn't that worth paying £20, £30, even £50 to get me?

DIRECT MARKETING

22

Pot-pourri

In all good lists, there is a section called 'miscellaneous', and in the case of direct marketing that section is probably more interesting, more innovative and more unusual than most. We've looked at media, letterbox and telephone as conventional opportunities to target pre-identified prospects, but what else is there? Well, in no particular order, here is a miscellany of alternatives.

PUBLICATION

If your industry hasn't got a magazine, or is not well served by a publication, publish your own! Make it look independent and authoritative, but tactically drop your own ads and inserts in. Ultimately, you can use direct marketing to sell subscriptions too!

CATALOGUES

We've talked about catalogues elsewhere, but you don't have to be in mail order to have a catalogue. You can use it as a promotional device as well.

Case Study

Whitbread

Product:

Vouchers to be redeemed in 12 different outlets.

Objectives:

1. To bring Whitbread Leisure Vouchers to the front of mind of agencies throughout the UK when considering incentives for a campaign.
2. To obtain an accurate list of account directors for future marketing use.

Target market:

Since there was no list of account directors, we mailed creative directors within agencies.

Offer:

£10 Whitbread Voucher for every four account directors recommended.

Creative platform:

Since creative directors are the most cynical of audiences, we had to produce a mailing that had significant impact. This involved sending a box with Hogarth-style illustrations on the front and the main headline 'Eat, Drink And Be Merry', emphasizing the benefits of Whitbread Leisure Vouchers.

Results:

10 per cent of those originally mailed responded.

MGM: MEMBER GET MEMBER, OR RAF: RECOMMEND A FRIEND (OR RAT ON A FRIEND)

Your customers will give you referrals – use them. Say 'thank you' with a reward. For example, split a case of wine between the recommender and the recommendee. Or give them as many entries in a free prize draw as the names they give you.

MARKET RESEARCH

Use direct mail for market research. Mail out a questionnaire to find out what people think about your product or service, or to find out why they are not buying any more. If you offer an incentive you will increase response. If you want to keep it anonymous, offer a donation to charity for every one returned.

You will get a higher response if you make your questionnaire attitudinal – more of an 'opinionnaire' – 'What do you think?', rather than 'What do you want to buy?' These are particularly useful for unconverted enquiries or lapsed customers.

FOLLOW-UPS

An unconverted enquiry or a non-responding name is potential for which you have already paid. There's no law saying they have to convert on our time frame. So mail them again… and again. Before you give up, make them a final offer, asking them why they're not responding.

INCENTIVES

Incentives are very important in direct marketing. You must first decide whether you are providing an incentive for a response or a sale, as that will affect the value of what you offer. Normally, you would offer for conversion, unless you want to build a lead file.

Case Study

Teltscher Bros

Product:

Three brands of liqueur – Bénédictine, Noilly Prat and De Kuyper Cherry Brandy.

Objectives:

To compile a customer database and use this to build customer loyalty and retention.

Target market:

Previous responders to promotions, visitors to Noilly Prat and Bénédictine distilleries not previously mailed.

Offers:

Free miniature liqueur and prize draw for a weekend in Paris, linked to MGM promotion to get names of up to three friends.

Creative platform:

A motivational questionnaire about drinking habits.

Channels/Media:

Direct mail to newly created database.

Results:

Response: 41 per cent; requested a sample to try: 90 per cent; recommended up to three friends: 81 per cent.

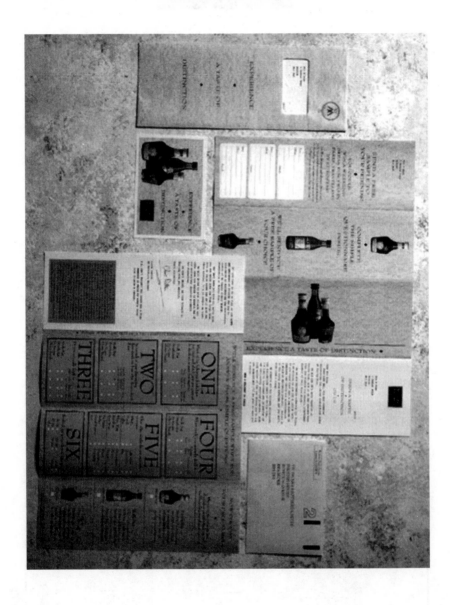

Broadly speaking, incentives can be divided into 'carrots' and 'cuddles'. Carrots are straight bribes. Cuddles – giving to a charity, gaining knowledge from a free guide or 'kit' – make the recipient feel better. Don't necessarily relate your gift to your premium. You don't have to offer a calculator just because you're selling a financial product. Look at what other people are offering. In the consumer market anything with a plug works well. Think about telephones, Filofaxes, holiday breaks and luggage.

In the business market, make sure that you offer something that is theoretically work-related, so it cannot be construed as a bribe or a high-value goodie that someone will take home.

Don't forget free prize draws. People love them and genuinely believe that they have a chance of winning. It also controls how much you are putting into your prize fund, whereas free gifts can get out of hand if you are over-subscribed.

CHRISTMAS CARDS

These can be part of direct marketing too. They offer another chance to put over your message, particularly if you do them humorously.

'WELL, IT WORKS FOR ME!'

Case Study

Hertz Leasing

Product:

Car-fleet leasing.

Objectives:

To generate leads from finance directors.

Challenges:

Fleet managers tend to have local loyalties and don't necessarily get the best deals. Finance directors care about money but would be completely switched off by discussions on cars per se.

Target market:

Finance directors of medium to large companies.

Offer:

Every year, Hertz commissions a major report into the fleet market – tax implications, preferred colours and makes, etc – and this is free to any finance director who will see the rep.

Creative platform:

Factual and featuring the report as hero.

Channels/Media:

Cold direct mail.

Results:

Very good.

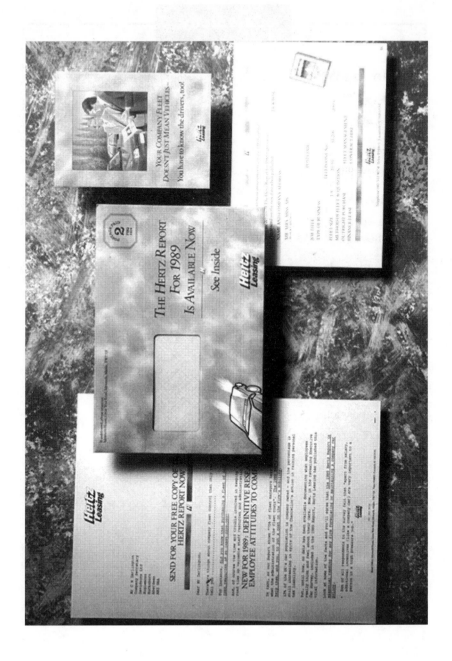

Littlewoods Catalogues

Product:

Home shopping.

Objectives:

To reactivate dormant agents.

Challenges:

Once an agent hasn't ordered for a period of time, the chances are she has switched catalogues, so getting her back is difficult.

Target market:

Existing agents.

Offer:

Free soft-toy puppies for the next three orders.

Creative platform:

Make the puppy the hero.

Channels/Media:

Direct mail to agents.

Results:

Excellent.

NEWSLETTERS

These are a very effective way of maintaining contact with customers and prospects. Keep them lively and well written, and provide some participation such as a competition or a letters page.

WRITE A BOOK

Well, I would say that, wouldn't I? But if you are seen as a specialist in your industry, why not?

There are surely many more ideas. These are just to whet your appetite and make you realize that direct marketing is whatever you want it to be!

CONCLUSION

It's no surprise that direct marketing is growing at the rate it is – because it works, it's measurable, it's accountable, and it's fun! There are many, many ways to do it. I hope this book has helped open your minds to the possibilities. The rest is down to you.

Good Luck!

Glossary

3-D Mailing: Something other than just paper.

Bangtail Envelopes: Reply envelopes with an extra large flap which can be torn off, completed, and inserted in the envelope.

Booster: An extra piece of paper in a mailpack which boosts response by promoting a particular message or making a specific offer.

Catalogue Pagination: Deciding which products go on which pages and how much page area they should have.

Cold Lists: A list you have to rent or buy with which you have no previous connections and on which are people who are not your customers.

CRM: Customer Relationship Management. Simply put, it's using the information you have on your customers to make them specific offers which make them more loyal.

DRTV: TV campaigns which generate a direct response.

E-Commerce: Can be electronic mail order or electronic advertising or electronic correspondence. Be sure you know which you want!

Follow-Ups: A chasing letter or phone call to a non-responder.

Johnson Box: A visual container for a letter headline consisting of a box of asterisks in which the message sits.

Laundry List: An order form which already has all the merchandise printed on it with boxes to tick for what to order.

Lift Letter: A second letter in a mailpack.

Loose Inserts: Card or paper inserted loose into a magazine or newspaper.

Merge/Purge: Running two or more lists against each other to identify and remove duplicates.

MGM/RAF: Member Get Member, Recommend A Friend. Getting a customer to give you a name and address of another possible customer.

Net Names: The names you are left to mail from a rented list after removing your existing customers.

Nixies/Goneaways: Mailings which are returned to the mailer because the recipient is no longer at that address.

Off the Page: An ad in a newspaper or magazine which asks for an order.

One Stage/One Step: Getting an immediate order or sale.

PPI: Postage Paid Impression. A pre-printed symbol on an envelope which shows it has effectively been 'stamped'.

Product Despatch: Putting your printed message in another business's mailing or parcel programme.

Profiling: Applying a code to an address which identifies the characteristics of that household or individual, based on accumulated data from surveys or other sources.

PSRs (Postal Sector Ranking): Lists of postal sectors for a door drop which match the profile required.

Response Mechanism: What you should have in all your direct marketing! Can be a card, a coupon, a phone number, a Web site. Ideally, you need to be able to track and measure it in detail.

Reverse Targeting: Using direct response activity to let the prospect identify themselves to you, rather than pre-identifying them.

SMEs: Small and Medium Enterprises – companies employing under 250, who are considered the engines of growth by Government.

Split Run: A head-to-head test of two different things – could be lists, headlines, free gifts – in mail or advertising, in order to determine which pulls better.

Targeting: Knowing in advance who you want to reach, defining that audience by characteristics and then using the characteristics to help the planning.

Tip-Ons: A reply card or other response device stuck on to a press or magazine ad.

Trace Codes: Used to measure parts of response – which list, which offer, which message – by putting a code on the piece that is returned.

Two Stage/Two Step: Getting an enquiry or expression of interest.

Warm Lists: Your own in-house list of customers and prospects.

Index

3-D mail   88, 189

ACORN   50–51, 54, 62
advertising *see* direct response
    advertising
air, in letters   75
Alliance & Leicester   107–09, 117–21
art, of direct marketing   1–6

bangtail envelopes   81, 189
benchmarks   173
Beneficial Bank   72–74, 86–87
benefits, of direct marketing   5
benefits, of your product   11
book-writing approach   188
boosters   80, 189
bouncebacks   18
bound-in inserts   123, 135
BP   68–69
BRAD (British Rate and Data)   105
Bradford & Bingley Building Society
    148–50
brand positioning   67
bribes   151, 183
British Fuels   97–98
British Rate and Data (BRAD)   105
brochures   77
BSkyB   89–90
BT   165–66
business lists   58–66

Cable London   27–28, 34–35
CAMEO UK   57
candidate media schedule   105
'carrot' incentives   183
catalogues   22–23, 164–72, 177
census data   50–51
'chance to win' approach   147
channels of communication   16–25
Christmas cards   183
classified ads   110, 127
cold lists   33–40, 189
    business   58–66
    consumer   41–49
communication by telephone   158
comparators   173
consumer benefits   11
consumer lists   41–49
copy for catalogues   171
corporate positioning   67
creative targeting   40
creatives   29, 67–76
    direct-response advertising
        110–11
    door-to-door   136, 139
CRM (customer relationship
    management)   189
'cuddles' incentives   183

Dairy Daughters   3–4

databases   95–103
definitions of direct marketing   1–6
Department of Trade and Industry
      162–63
dial-for-details   159
direct mail   16–17, 26–32
   content   77–84
   creativity   67–76
   databases   95–103
   as a tactile medium   85–94
   see also lists
directories   61
direct-response advertising   17,
      104–14
   generating response   127–35
   media buying   115–16
direct-response television (DRTV)
      114, 189
display ads   110, 127
door-to-door   17–18, 136–39
Drive Computing   145–46
DRTV (direct-response television)
      114, 189

e-commerce   22, 160–63, 189
EDs (Enumeration Districts)   50–51,
      54
electoral roll   45–46
Employment Department   129–30
enquirer lists   41–42
envelopes   70–71
exclusivity   144, 147
exhibition attendee lists   61
eye movement patterns   170

F (frequency) data   99
Family Assurance Society   124–25
follow-ups   180, 189

'free' telephone numbers   158–59
frequency (F) data   99

glossary   189–91
goneaways   66, 190

headlines
   advertisements   128, 131
   letters   75
Heather Valley   168–69
Hertz Leasing   184–85
horizontal readership   61–62
hot spots (of catalogues)   167, 170

incentives   180–83
inserts   123, 131–32, 135
Internet   22, 160–63

Johnson box   75, 189

KISS formula   29

Lakeland Limited   154–56
'last-chance' questionnaires   103
Late Cards   123
'laundry list' order forms   81, 190
Leeds Visa   47–48
letters   75–76, 80
lifestyle lists   46
lifetime value   176
lift letters   80, 190
list brokers   33
list houses   33, 36–37
list managers   33
list owners   33
listening skills   158
lists   29, 33–40
   business   58–66